SNAP, CRACKLE,
AND
POPULAR TASTE

SNAP, CRACKLE, AND POPULAR TASTE

*The Illusion of Free Choice
in America*

Jeffrey Schrank

A DELTA ORIGINAL

A DELTA ORIGINAL

Published by
Dell Publishing Co., Inc.
1 Dag Hammarskjold Plaza
New York, New York 10017

ISBN: 0-440-57155-3

Printed in the United States of America
Second printing

ACKNOWLEDGMENTS

"Southbound on the Freeway" by May Swenson: reprinted by permission of the author
from *To Mix with Time*, copyright © 1963 by May Swenson.

Dialogue from radio commercial used courtesy California Prune Advisory Board.

VB

CONTENTS

SNAP, CRACKLE,
AND
POPULAR TASTE

INTRODUCTION

This book is about the seemingly insignificant decisions in daily life. It is about watching television, shopping, reading ads, playing sports and other everyday activities that fill so much of a life span. *Snap, Crackle, and Popular Taste* is concerned more with what you might choose for breakfast tomorrow morning or with how you travel to work each day than with carefully constructed decisions to adopt a career, get married or join a commune. The book examines some of the hidden factors that shape everyday decisions and our experience of freedom.

Freedom exists only in the presence of choices, but it does not follow that the presence of choices creates freedom. Some choices contribute only to the illusion of freedom; these we will call pseudo-choices. A pseudo-choice should not be confused with the absence of choice. A pseudo-choice is a real choice exercised by a person using what is commonly recognized as free will, but the choice has carefully controlled boundaries that often exclude what the person choosing really wants.

For example, I might develop a sudden craving for a lemon cream pie. Thanks to modern technology I am able to race down to the local supermarket, pick out my pie and have it ready to eat as soon as it thaws a bit. What I wanted was a lemon cream pie such as my memory told me Mother used to make. What I bought was a box showing a picture of a lemon cream pie and containing a collection of water and chemicals utterly devoid of lemons or cream. But I eat the pie with a certain degree of enjoyment because I have learned to be satisfied with what is offered instead of with what I wanted. This is pseudo-choice.

While I was at the supermarket I picked up a box of Screaming Yellow Zonkers, a new kind of double-edged razor blade and my first package of chewing gum in six years. I'm not sure why I bought these things, but they're small and I'll use them. This, too, is pseudo-choice. It is pseudo-choice not because I acted on impulse but because I was unaware of the carefully constructed decision/environment that encouraged me to add these purchases.

Pseudo-choice is a selection guided by invisible limitations and structures. It is the invisibility of the decision-shaping factors that contributes to pseudo-choice. It is tempting to believe that choosing among the dazzling array of options offered is freedom. In pseudo-choice, the world is a multiple-choice test. We are free to answer questions only in terms of the options presented. A real-choice test would have only blank space for our answers which would be unshaped by the test maker. A multiple-choice test offers real choices but only the illusion of freedom.

A strong case can be made for the fact that the illusion of freedom is all we really desire. The case has been best presented by Erich Fromm in *Escape from Freedom*. Real freedom, Fromm observes, is a heavy burden, loaded with responsibility and far too painful for the average person to bear. Pseudo-choice services nicely to create the illusion of freedom and preserve us from the introspection needed to determine what we really want.

One reason freedom has become increasingly susceptible to control is that it has changed its meaning in the popular mind. Freedom has increasingly become associated with a feeling rather than a state of being. The noun "freedom" has become a verb. Freedom is no longer a fragile state of being or a goal to pursue with lifelong struggle and desire, it is a feeling that can come and go like fear, sadness or boredom. To "feel free" has replaced to "be free" both in common vocabulary and in the list of goals worth attaining. Ads and mass media reinforce this situation by associating products ranging from bras to cigars, from motorcycles to carpet cleaners, with the feeling of freedom. Feelings are relatively easy to manipulate compared to a state of being, living conditions or social structures. If freedom is a feeling, a rush of exhilaration, it can be briefly satisfied by consumer products and packaged entertainments. Pseudo-choice can contribute to the illusion of freedom while obscuring the lack of true freedom.

Pseudo-choices can be characterized in the following ways:

1. They are presented to the individual as a part of a mass—an audience, a consumer or potential customer. In the marketplace, objects of potential pseudo-choice are made for "anyone," and not for someone in particular.

2. They often consist of a set of carefully controlled options. Almost everyone who shops at a supermarket comes out with bags of food, half of which was produced by the ten leading food companies.

3. The factors shaping the choices are invisible to most people.

4. They tend to obscure (but not necessarily obliterate) real choices. In purchasing an automobile, there are so many options offered that real choices in safety and ease of maintenance are rarely considered.

5. Pseudo-choices are often supported by advertising or public relations efforts which invariably attempt to make them appear far more significant than they are.

6. They are preselected, controlled choices that tend to prevent people from asking the basic question: "What do I really want?" By so doing, they contribute to the state of general detachment and help create large numbers of people who simply don't know what they want. And those who don't know what they want are the most easily satisfied with pseudo-choice.

Pseudo-choice is related to Jacques Ellul's concept of sociological propaganda, as distinguished from political propaganda. Political propaganda is what is normally thought of when the word "propaganda" is used. It is an attempt by a government, a party, an administration or a pressure group to change the behavior of the public. The word "behavior" is carefully chosen since one of the misconceptions about propaganda is that it attempts to change beliefs rather than behavior.

Sociological propaganda is more diffuse. In *Propaganda: The Foundation of Men's Attitudes*, Ellul defines it as ". . . the penetration of an ideology by means of its sociological context." He sees such propaganda as

> . . . based on a general climate, an atmosphere that influences people imperceptibly without having the appearance of propaganda; it gets to man through his customs, through his most unconscious habits. It creates new habits in him; it is a sort of persuasion from within. As a result, man adopts new criteria of judgment and choice, adopts them spontaneously, as if he had chosen them himself.

The illusion of freedom is one of the "messages" of sociological propaganda and pseudo-choice is one of its techniques.

Alvin Toffler, in his book *Future Shock*, is critical of sociologists (including Ellul) and historians who see the limitation of choice as part of a bleak future. He contends instead that, ". . . the people of the future may suffer not from an absence of choice, but from a paralyzing surfeit of it. They may turn out to be victims of that peculiarly super-industrial dilemma: 'overchoice.' " Toffler points to the diversity in cigarette brands, gasoline, grocery store items, automobiles, etc. as proof of overchoice. In reality, as we shall see in the course of this book, these are examples of pseudo-choice that offer the illusion of free choice instead of a product that best serves the user.

In housing, for example, Toffler points out that as soon as the building industry improves its technology by increasing the use of standardized parts, we can expect a paradise of diversity in home design. He fails to realize that home design is already quite standardized and most of the elements of a house are mass produced. One company even offers a computer printout that acts as a detailed pattern, down to showing exactly where each nail is to be placed. Instead of introducing real diversity and genuine "custom design" (the word "custom" has become one of the most common euphemisms for pseudo-choice), houses seem to be increasingly poured from the same few molds with choices limited to the trimmings. One can have a house with pieces of wood nailed on the outside called Tudor, or one with an overhanging roof called French or one with white pillars attached to the front roof over-hang and called Colonial. But you cannot choose a house exactly suited to your own family's life-style unless you can afford the expense and time to build a real custom house.

Toffler is correct in pointing out that success in technology can be measured in terms of consumer acceptance. But acceptance cannot be adequately measured by the most often used statistics of ratings and sales. People need to be asked if they thoroughy enjoy the house they live in, if they really want to watch TV tonight or do so merely because there is nothing else to do, if they really enjoy the taste of those frozen dinners or eat them because they appear cheap and require so little time.

This book does not contend that Americans no longer have freedom of choice or that big business is running our lives down to the last detail. There are real choices offered. Options are avail-able, but these require effort to seek out and often a willingness to risk. It is still possible to find tasty and nutritious food in stores, to locate a house designed for human living and even to experience true recreation in the mass media.

The following chapters are not a consideration of the problem of free choice in society. They are not essays in philosophy, politics or history. Instead, they concentrate on the mundane, everyday aspects of life. Other writers have dealt with the larger question of a free society and the possibility or futility of finding freedom and order in the universe. This book is based on the belief that aware-ness of the many pseudo-choices in daily life will help the reader better realize the need for alternatives. *Snap, Crackle, and Popular Taste* is a book intended to raise awareness levels about everyday decisions. It does not offer solutions to contradictions in society, recipes for increasing one's sense of freedom or advice on beating the pseudo-choice game in the supermarket.

Pseudo-choice is not the only concern of this book. It is also an examination of some important but rarely analyzed aspects of daily life. On the pages that follow we will be examining the food we eat, the means we use to travel, the advertising that is a constant part of the environment, television, popular taste, the culture of the marketplace, institutions and the use of leisuretime.

Chapter 1

There Are No Mass Media: All We Have Is Television

The problem with television is that the people must sit and keep their eyes glued on a screen; the average American family hasn't time for it. Therefore, the showmen are convinced that for this reason, if for no other, television will never be a serious competitor of broadcasting.
> —*The New York Times*, March 19, 1939. A reporter evaluating a new invention seen at the World's Fair.

"You might just as well say," added the March Hare, "that 'I like what I get' is the same thing as 'I get what I like.' "
> —a well-known rabbit speaking to Alice somewhere in Wonderland

Score one for the rabbit in this battle of insight between the March Hare and *The New York Times*. Thirty years after *The Times* reporter dismissed TV as merely another novelty of the 1939 World's Fair, a Gallup poll revealed that Americans rank television as their "favorite evening pastime." In the voting for most popular activity, Americans cast ballots by turning TV knobs and dials and have selected to settle for liking what they get rather than getting what they like.

For the average American (an admittedly elusive creature bearing some resemblance to a unicorn), watching television consumes more time than any other single activity except sleep. In millions of households, bedtime itself is determined by the end of the late night news or the *TV Guide* announcement of who will substitute for Johnny Carson. Even toilet habits are regimented by television, at least according to a discovery made by the Lafayette, Louisiana, water department.

While the rest of the city watches TV, the employees at the water department watch gauges and needles that are far less exciting than even the dullest of programs. Perhaps the boredom of the work gave rise to the introduction of a TV set into the water gauge room. However it happened, someone noticed that the graph used to gauge water pressure took noticeable dips during commercials and at the end of TV shows. The observation gave rise to the waterwork's own version of the Nielsen ratings.

The water department reported that the movie *Airport* produced a record drop of twenty-six pounds per square inch. The department observed that "at approximately 8:30 a bomb exploded in the airplane and from then until 9:00, when the pilot landed safely and the movie ended, almost nobody left their television set to do anything . . . then the 26-pound drop." The regimented toilet break led to twenty-thousand people flushing at the same time, using about eighty thousand gallons of water. The same scene was undoubtedly repeated across the nation as television gave the orders for what resembled a heartless joke played by an all-powerful but unseen dictator.

Synchronized flushing is anything but the most important effect of television on national behavior patterns, but it does illustrate the difficulty of measuring or even realizing how TV influences behavior. We do know that by the time a typical American reaches the deathbed (appropriately placed underneath a TV set in a hospital room), he or she will have spent nearly seven years watching television. Without television, seven years would be added to the average person's activity-life. It is difficult to believe that we have freely chosen to spend so much of a lifetime watching dancing phosphers on a two-dimensional screen. In its young lifetime, television has so dominated American life that the decision to watch has itself become a pseudo-choice.

For millions of regular viewers, television is no longer one option from among a vast array of choices to occupy a weekday night. The option has become *which* programs to watch, not *if* the set should be on. On any given weekday night, year after year, no matter what programs are presented, there is a fairly constant TV audience in about thirty to forty million of the nation's sixty-seven million households. Instead of a freely chosen occasional diversion, tele-viewing has become a habit, an addiction requiring a nightly fix. In his book, *The Americans*, historian Daniel Boorstin comments on the relation of the citizen to the TV:

> *Television watching became an addiction comparable only to life itself. If the set was not on, Americans began to feel that they had missed what was "really happening. . . ." And just as it was axiomatic that it was better to be alive than to be dead, so it became axiomatic that it was better to be watching something than to be watching nothing at all. When there was "nothing on TV tonight," there was a painful void.*

To call televiewing an addiction is not merely to employ a figure of speech for shock effect. Addiction, normally associated with drug usage, has two necessary components—tolerance and a with-drawal illness or abstinence syndrome. "Tolerance" is the gradual adaption of the body to the drug (or substance) so that more and more is required to produce the same effect previously obtained with a smaller dosage. A "withdrawal illness" is an adverse physi-cal reaction to a complete lack of the addicting substance, while "abstinence syndrome" refers to usually minor symptoms (run-ning nose, sweating, tremors, irritability, etc.) when the normal dosage is delayed or missed.

These two elements of addiction can both be seen in viewing habits. The component of tolerance can be seen in the gradual increase of the "average daily dosage" self-prescribed by viewers over the past eleven years. The average household in 1963 had the set on for five hours and twelve minutes; by 1974 that figure had increased to six hours and fourteen minutes and has remained almost unchanged since then.

The addiction component of withdrawal can be seen in the millions who rush to have the TV set repaired (or rent a replacement) as soon as it breaks and in those who experience boredom and irritation on those evenings when "nothing's on". Perhaps the best illustration of the addictive nature of televiewing can be found in the experiment conducted by the Society for Rational Psychology in Germany. One hundred eighty-four volunteers were paid to give up television for one year. After a brief period during which the subjects reported happily spending more time with their children, reading, visiting relatives and playing more games, the withdrawal symptoms struck. Tension and quarreling increased dramatically, even wife-beating reached a new intensity and the volunteers' sexual activity declined. Not one lasted more than five months in a state of tubelessness. Once the sets were restored, the symptoms disappeared.

Henner Ertel, one of the psychologists who conducted the experiment, attributed the results to the fact that, "Television tends to cover up conflicts between habitual viewers. Many behavior patterns become so closely linked to TV that they are negatively influenced if one takes the set away. The problem is that of addiction." Television, much like marijuana and alcohol, is a kind of addictive buffer. It allows people who have only superficialities in common to be together in a form of peace and seeming contentment. Or, as T. S. Eliot observed, "Television is the medium which permits millions of people to listen to the same joke at the same time and yet remain lonesome."

If television has become the "opiate of the masses," as many of its critics contend, it is no surprise that it should usurp some of the functions traditionally served by religion. Symbolic of the role of TV as electronic religion are several TV towers, two-fifths of a mile high, on the Midwestern prairies. From the towers of Babylon through medieval church steeples and Indian totem poles, cultures have built their tallest structures to demonstrate their deepest beliefs. In the United States, the tallest buildings are those given to business, but the tallest structures are television transmitting towers.

Televiewing is a ritual activity that can be seen as forming part of a common symbolic environment whose true predecessor is religion. The celebrities are the priests of the videosphere, the three networks its denominations (with PBS a mild case of schism and video freaks potential heretics), and the rating system its morality and ethics. The TV sets and antennae are the shrines and altars, and its ritual is the utter regularity of programs viewed at the foot of the glass box shrine. The worship service is outlined as strictly as in any religion by a set of rubrics printed in the weekly *TV Guide*—the nation's largest selling magazine.

Considering television as a partial fulfillment of the need for ritual helps explain the presence of so much repetition in TV series, ads and reruns—repetition is at the heart both of propaganda and of ritual. Perhaps we are like the African tribe who reportedly saw *King Kong* as its first movie. When the film ended there were resounding cheers. The next week they were again shown a movie, but this time they tore down the tent, the screen and attacked the projector because the film was not *King Kong*. Upon hearing this story Robert Goldfarb, then director of program development for CBS, commented, "Maybe people do want to see the same thing week in and week out."

The fact that television series, year after year, are basically the same stories with updated characters and situations supports the belief that TV is watched as a ritual habit. Adventure series celebrate the conquest of evil by the forces of goodness, and the hero with 1001 faces can be seen any night on all the channels. According to Richard Carpenter of the Center for the Study of Popular Culture at Bowling Green State University,

> *Such a pattern, repeated night after night in dozens of versions all portraying the same basic theme, implies that the TV audience derives satisfaction from a ritual formalization of ingrained feelings that the evil in the world can be overcome by men working together under the guidance of a leader. The overwhelming complexities of individuals and social problems are simplified and brought within a manageable compass.*

Such is the scholarly language of the academic "discipline" of pop culture. An anthropologist might remind us in somewhat simpler language that TV programs reaffirm tribal values. But the most concise statement of the role of TV as religion is media historian Erik Barnouw's reminder that "TV entertainment is propaganda for the status quo."

Further evidence for televiewing as a ritual activity that depends little on which specific programs are shown from year to year is offered by Paul Klein, former vice-president for audience measurement at NBC. He claims that programming is based on the Theory of the Least Objectionable Program. According to the LOP theory, people don't watch particular programs—they watch television. The set is turned on for the same reason people climb mountains—it's there. The program viewed is the one that at that time is the least objectionable. The LOP theory explains why some interesting programs die and stupid ones live on. "Place a weak show against weaker competition, LOP teaches, and it inevitably looks good." Network programmers know that some well-received programs are stupid, but they also know that a program doesn't have to be good, "it only has to be less objectionable than whatever the hell the other guys throw against it." Thus "Marcus Welby" was watched instead of "First Tuesday" because "When a girl has syphilis on 'Welby,' we can expect a happy ending. When the same girl has it on 'First Tuesday,' we expect to catch it."

Our language further supports Paul Klein's LOP theory in that we read *the* newspaper, listen to *the* radio, read *a* book or *a* magazine but simply watch television. There is some truth buried in this linguistic habit, for we do watch the medium of television and that is significant no matter if the program is opera or mystery.

The Least Objectionable Program theory is another way of saying that televiewing is a pseudo-choice. It should be clear that not every decision to watch TV is a pseudo-choice; but television is so used by society that much, if not most, viewing falls into the pseudo-choice category.

The LOP theory could be adapted and applied to the automobile to produce the LOMT (Least Objectionable Means of Transportation) theory which states that people don't really choose to spend so much time in automobiles, they simply find autos the least objectionable choice available. The Least Offensive Food theory holds that the highly processed "convenience foods" are not chosen for their taste or goodness but because they have been presented as the least offensive.

Pseudo-choice is a kind of psychological Ohm's Law, a tendency to follow the path of least offensiveness. That such choices exist is not a new phenomenon, but that such choices are so widely confused with free choice is a disturbing tendency. Those who consider these choices in autos, food and TV "free choices" need to be reminded by some contemporary version of the March Hare that, "You might as well say that I like what I get is the same thing as I get what I like."

Television watching falls easily into the area of pseudo-choice because it seems such an inconsequential decision. But each choice to watch has hidden consequences implicit. Each decision to watch includes a hidden or pseudo-choice not to engage with living people, not to take part in any other active process, and to allow a handful of corporate executives to assume responsibility for one's own recreation. The decision to watch also contains a secondary choice to subject oneself to a certain kind of value-laden education and conditioning. This educational aspect of *all* television works very slowly but with an inevitability matched only by its invisibility. Perhaps the most important hidden educational function of television is that of emotional education.

Consider television and the situation Plato describes in Book Seven of his *Republic*. Plato presents the parable of the four prisoners chained together in a cave since childhood. They face a wall filled with shadows cast by the light from a fire behind them. All they know of the world is the shadows. One of the prisoners is released and realizes that the shadows he took for the world are only imitations of a far greater reality. He returns to share this discovery with the other prisoners but is rejected as a heretic. The prisoners are incapable of distinguishing between the shadows and reality.

Plato's allegory takes on a new dimension in a society that experiences many emotions in a darkened movie house or the euphemistically named family room where the TV is enthroned. Like the prisoners, we too spend much time watching shadows that flicker across a screen. We too sometimes have problems distinguishing the shadows from reality, depending partly on how much time we spend in the electronic cave.

We have all experienced deep emotions in front of TV screens; we have all learned about the world we will never visit in person or experience "live." We watch television in order to be manipulated into feeling. We want those shadows on the screen to be frightening, to make us cry or howl with laughter, to help us feel vicarious thrills and excitement, to stimulate awe at the ability of others. Our nervous systems do not distinguish between the fear of a mugger lurking ahead on the deserted street at three in the morning or the fear aroused by the midnight creature feature. In both cases our heart throbs, the pulse quickens and the body sensations are real. The feelings are real, only the televised stimulus is lacking a third dimension.

People have always sought out games and theater to experience feelings normally missing from daily life. But when the seeking takes six to eight hours a day it is a sign of an absence of a rich emotional life based on reality. The shadows become substitutes for reality. A Los Angeles soap opera addict explains: "Without these programs going on, I wonder if I would go on. People seem to forget me. . . . These people are my company. My real friends. I have it [TV] on because I feel people are talking to me."

This woman is an extreme case of TV-as-reality-substitute, but her symptoms are common to millions. By watching television, the feelings and sense of companionship can be enjoyed without responsibility, without the need to share these feelings with others or express them in public or even to "own" them as ours. These TV-generated feelings come from skilled writers and producers and not from within ourselves—they are safe and nonthreatening. Television encourages habitual viewers to abdicate responsibility for their own recreation and feelings of aliveness. Responsibility slips into the willing hands of corporations who control TV content as well as the supply of goods presented as means to "come alive."

True, these same feelings can be experienced by leaving the electronic cave, but risks must be taken to seek them out and their effects must be faced. Inside the cave TV acts upon viewers as a mass, as part of an audience they are objects to be acted upon. The shadows in the cave are projected in order to play upon emotions; they are clear, simple stimuli which demand only those patterned responses we have all learned so well from so much time spent with TV. Time devoted to watching television teaches how to respond to video realities. This is what Marshall McLuhan meant by "the medium is the message." It is not so important *what* we watch, as it is *that* we watch.

Video critic Gene Youngblood contrasts the commercial entertainer with the artist and sheds light on why we watch so much entertainment television:

> By perpetuating a destructive habit of unthinking response to formulas, by forcing us to rely ever more frequently on memory, the commercial entertainer encourages an unthinking response to daily life, inhibiting self-awareness . . . He offers nothing we haven't already conceived, nothing we don't already expect. Art explains, entertainment exploits. Entertainment gives us what we want; art gives us what we don't know we want.

Robert Hunter in *The Storming of the Mind* proposes that these shadowy images have taught us the unprecedented ability to respond to the unreal as though it were real. We have watched so much television that we have come to expect life to be as clear and neatly packaged as the prime-time shows.

Exactly how television has influenced our psychology we don't know, for we are all still living in the cave of the electronic image. Even if we spend little time watching the shadows ourselves, our fellow prisoners make up a society profoundly influenced by television. We have yet to find an escapee to report back to us on what life would be like in twentieth-century America without television. Truly scientific studies on the psychological effects of television are difficult to construct. In order to conduct such studies, one would need a group of non-TV viewers and a control group of TV viewers alike in as many ways as possible with the single exception of TV habits. But those who shun television are such a statistical minority and atypical that they have to be classified as "abnormal" and thus not subject to control groups. Another possibility would be to find some remote community within the United States that has little or no access to TV signals. Unfortunately, there is no such isolated, TV-free community. About the best a researcher could do in the contiguous United States is the Apache Indian Reservation in Arizona where *only* 81 percent of the "households" have a television.

In the face of a lack of hard evidence, we turn to educated guesses and surveys. A professional polling organization conducted a survey of the attitude of readers of the *National Enquirer* toward television. Of the responders, 76 percent agreed that "TV makes me feel tired," 75 percent agreed that it "makes me eat more," 56 percent claimed that TV causes them to "sleep more," and two-thirds agreed that TV leads to "less sex." Less than a majority of viewers polled rated entertainment programs as "satisfactory." Yet this box in the living room that shows mainly unsatisfactory programs and makes viewers hungry, sleepy and sexless is one of the few experiences in American life that nearly all people have in common.

We suspect that box for causing problems even without proof beyond a reasonable doubt. When we discover that high-school and college students can no longer write an English sentence, the experts suggest television as part culprit. Jerzy Kosinski, whose novel *Being There* dealt with the relation between TV and reality, suggests that TV has crippled students. In an interview he indicates that the effects of TV can be easily seen : "Go into any high school and see how limited students' perception of themselves is, how crippled their imaginations, how unable they are to tell a story, to read or concentrate, or even to describe an event accurately a moment after it happens. See how easily they are bored, how quickly they take up the familiar 'reclining' position in the classroom, how short their attention span is."

Before they enter formal schooling, children watch "Sesame Street" and learn the value of being regular and heavy consumers of TV programming. They also learn to accept as normal the fast cutting of "Sesame Street" and fail to learn the value of watching any one scene or visual for more than a few seconds. Producers of filmstrips for high-school students now find that they can leave a single picture on the screen only for an average of eight seconds or else students become bored. TV has taught the desirability of frequent change and the method of coping with what is undesirable by "changing channels."

Los Angeles psychiatrist Dr. Lawrence Friedman explains one tendency of the channel-changing personality: "I'm convinced that at least fifty percent of all divorces in this country are unnecessary. And it's all because TV teaches us simple solutions to complex problems. People tell me: 'If only I could get rid of this marriage, everything would be all right.' Nonsense!"

We don't know with any degree of scientific certainty if TV shares the blame for a decline in writing and reading skills or the increase in the divorce rate. But there have been some carefully conducted studies that provide clues. Although unmeasurable, the most pervasive effect of television is that it is an invention that causes the majority of citizens to spend a huge portion of their lives as passive spectators instead of as participants in an active process. Some indication of the link between passivity and TV viewing can be seen in a study based on an idea of Erich Fromm.

Fromm used the phrases biophilia and necrophilia to label tendencies in human nature. Both tendencies are inherent in each individual but one is usually dominant. Biophilic people are drawn to that which is alive, growing, free and unpredictable. They tend to avoid violence and that which destroys life, including mechanization in living patterns. They enjoy a wide variety of life experiences rather than seek out extraordinary excitement or thrills.

Necrophilics are attracted to what is dead, mechanical and rigidly ordered. Necrophilics believe that force is needed to control people. Since they often feel dead (bored) inside, they seek thrills to provide shots of excitement.

Psychoanalyst Michael Maccoby tested the theory that necrophilics would be more attracted to television than biophilics. He sampled five hundred mothers of high-school-age children in California. First the women were given a test of projective questions to measure their bio/necrophilic tendencies. Then the amount of time each spent watching television was surveyed. The study showed that necrophilia is significantly more present among those who watch much television than among those who seldom watch TV. Of the mothers classified as more biophilic, only 27 percent watched more than seven hours a week. Of those grouped in the necrophilic category, 65 percent watched from eight to fifty-six hours weekly.

Other circumstantial evidence of the effects of television comes from Stanley Stern at the USC School of Education. He conducted studies to measure the influence of television on children's creativity. He found that children who regularly watched any kind of programs (even educational) on TV during the three-week test period showed a lowering of test scores. Only the group who received no special instructions about watching TV showed consistent improvement in creativity as measured by a standardized test. Those who did watch television showed a notable decrease in all areas except verbal ability. Cartoons had the worst effect overall, but even educational programs lowered creativity scores. Stern's conclusions are tentative but he does speculate that the passive nature of TV viewing is an important factor. "It is the act of engaging with living people," he believes, "that promotes intellectual benefits."

Russell Weigel and Richard Jessor studied the relation of TV viewing and adolescent conventionality. They found that more conventional adolescents (measured in terms of values, independence, reported behaviors, liberalism-conservatism) watch more TV. Unconventionality is not the same as creativity, but the results are tempting to conclude that watching television has negative social and psychological effects.

Passivity is especially significant as a cultural-conditioning factor in children. According to Bruno Bettelheim, who has worked extensively with autistic children, "Children who have been taught, or conditioned to listen passively most of the day to the warm verbal communication coming from the TV screen, the deep emotional appeal of the so-called TV personality, are often unable to respond to real persons because they arouse so much less feeling than the skilled actor. Worse, they lose the ability to learn from reality because life experiences are more complicated than the ones they see on the screen. . . . This being seduced into passivity and discouraged about facing life actively on one's own is the real danger of TV."

But can you prove that, Bruno? There is evidence to suggest that television promotes certain kinds of activity rather than passivity. The surgeon general has not yet required all TV sets to carry the warning, "This invention might be hazardous to your health," but he has concluded that "televised violence does indeed have an adverse effect on those children predisposed to violence and *no one knows how many children are 'predisposed.'* " To prove that TV promotes passivity is difficult, and most of the recent studies have attempted to show TV does or does not promote violence. Sometimes stories are more convincing than scientific experiments.

In 1966, NBC aired the film *The Doomsday Flight*, about a man who plants a bomb aboard an airplane and phones the airline offering to disclose its location upon payment of a ransom. Before the program ended one bomb threat was received, and by the end of the week a dozen had been reported by the major airlines—an increase of 800 percent over the previous month. When the film was televised in Australia, Qantas Airways lost $50,000 in ransom shortly thereafter in an event paralleling the plot of the film.

A woman in Boston's Roxbury ghetto was doused with gasoline and burned to death shortly after the first telecasting of the film *Fuzz* in which a similar act of violence takes place. Boston's chief of police blamed the example set by the film in spite of the fact that the scene was edited for television to lessen its impact.

A fourteen-year-old boy in Syracuse, a sort of child prodigy in electronics, copied techniques he saw on "Mission Impossible" to commit a series of robberies with a sophistication that would qualify him for the thieves' hall of fame. He was caught only because a friend blew the whistle.

In Los Angeles, a housemaid caught a seven-year-old boy in the act of sprinkling ground glass into the family's lamb stew. There was no malice behind the act; it was purely an experiment to see if it would really work as well as it did on television.

Crime and violence are recurring subjects that serve an educational purpose in the religion of television in which all programming is part of the sermon. Crime programs teach citizens the meaning of good and evil, how to behave when witnessing violence, who is likely to be a criminal and what death is like. A study of what is taught by prime-time violence shows that it leaves little room for reality to interfere.

Joseph Dominick, an assistant professor of communication at Queen's College in New York, and seven assistants monitored a week of prime-time TV and found that criminals were predominantly male (85 percent), twenty to fifty years old (78 percent) and white (90 percent). TV crime, Dominick found, "appears to be a white collar occupation committed primarily by specialists or by people with middle class occupations." On TV no one under twenty was arrested, and only 7 percent of those taken into custody are nonwhite. In reality, 35 percent of those arrested are under twenty and 30 percent are nonwhite. On TV only 7 percent of the total violence is committed on relatives, in reality this accounts for 25 to 30 percent. In reality, most murderers know their victims; on television, the stranger is more likely to kill.

TV criminals have to be as nondescript as possible to avoid any charges of racial or ethnic stereotyping. The most common TV crimes are murder, assault and armed robbery. Outside TVland, quiet burglaries, clever larcenies and unspectacular auto thefts are the big three. Video detectives solve 90 percent of their cases, just a bit more than real-life crime solvers.

A study of all the leading characters in prime-time TV found that more than half (241 of 445 in two weeks) inflict violence in some form upon other persons. Most of the violent encounters (eight out of ten) are between clearly identifiable "good guys" and "bad guys." Nearly half of all the leading characters who kill and more than half of all leading characters who are violent achieve a clearly happy ending in their episodes. The study found that half of all violent episodes do not involve witnesses. When present, witnesses are usually passive, not intervening. In the rare instance in which a witness does intervene, it is as often to encourage or assist violence as it is to prevent it. Lawful arrest and trial are shown as consequences of major acts of violence in only two out of every ten violent programs.

Physical pain is shown to be a consequence of violence in only one of every four violent acts. In television drama, violence does not hurt too much, nor are its consequences very bloody or messy, even though it may lead to death. Death is rarely shown in other than a violent context and is rarely presented realistically. Death is often a dramatic device used only as an excuse to eliminate a character or to introduce a California homicide department.

All this misinformation about crime and violence tends to teach fear of the anonymous stranger. Major crimes such as corporate law-avoidance, political corruption and misleading advertising receive relatively little TV time. People robbing banks makes for far more interesting stories than banks robbing people. But there is another, more pervasive message taught by violent programming. The occasional TV-provoked imitations of violent behavior can be seen as an unfortunate side effect of the more important violence education. Corporations would hardly sponsor programs that taught their workers and customers to steal, kill or commit crimes.

The violent programs carry an overall message that reaffirms the existing power structure and pockets of authority. According to George Gerbner, TV researcher and professor at the University of Pennsylvania, the message of violent programs is "one of social typing: different types of people possess different degrees of human violability." He sees this as part of training to indoctrinate people into killing simply because there is a type of people called by the government "enemy." If a populace no longer believes that "bad guys" need be killed, then military power as the ultimate weapon is undermined.

Symbolic violence on the tube also creates and channels fear among viewers. Gerbner's research has found that heavy TV viewers under the age of thirty are more fearful of life's dangers than their elders. Young women are the most fearful. And the reason for the fear could have something to do with the fact that they are the most victimized group on TV. For every twenty-one male killers, there are ten male victims. But there are fifteen female victims for every ten female killers.

Gerbner summarizes his views by observing that fearful people will demand protection and perhaps accept oppression in the name of safety. He says, "Our research shows that heavy viewing of television cultivates a sense of risk and danger in real life. Fear invites aggression that provokes still more fear and repression. The pattern of violence on TV may thus bolster a structure of social controls even as it appears to threaten it."

While not all programs contain violence and crime, they still educate and supply images to reinforce the status quo. Consider the lowly soap opera. These daytime TV minidramas are watched at some time by 76 percent of all nonworking women. The characters in the soaps are created to invite identification by the largely white, female, middle-class audience.

One soap opera writer was asked why so few working-class people appear on the soaps. He answered, "It's more interesting for a woman to see herself as a doctor's or lawyer's wife." But in soapland, crises are so common and shattering that viewers feel themselves lucky to have escaped paralysis, amnesia and a divorce all at once.

M. L. Ramsdell of Rollins College sat through six hundred hours of eight soap operas offered by one network in 1971-72. He found that in soapland the "good life" can be achieved by anybody who is a white male professional or a white female who marries the professional and, subsequently, becomes a "mommy." In one program, 90 percent of the primary male characters are either doctors or lawyers. Of the fifty-seven primary female roles, only eight were professionals. Soap housewives are almost always fulfilled, while workingwomen are frustrated. Some problems, such as illegitimacy, divorce and death, are handled with some degree of realism, Ramsdell found. Others, like old age, are hardly touched upon. He concludes that the soaps help to promote unrealizable expectations—that men need a professional degree to attain self-respect and happiness.

With television to provide so much misinformation, one would suspect that those who watch TV most are also those most misinformed about the world. Again the research of George Gerbner provides some proof that this might indeed be true. He has found through testing that those who watch TV the most have distorted conceptions about crime and its victims, workingwomen, minorities, job opportunities and medicine.

He found that 11.3 percent more heavy viewers than light viewers overestimated the percentage of world population comprising Americans, and 14.4 percent more heavy viewers than light viewers overestimated the percentage of white Americans employed as professionals and managers. Sex, age and schooling made no difference in results. Gerbner emphasizes the importance of the fact that heavy viewers significantly overestimate the incidence of violence and their own chances of encountering it in real life. "In order to have violence, you have to train victims, and engender a climate of fear."

A vastly simplified version of Gerbner's test is presented here to test your own degree of distortion:

TESTING YOUR DISTORTION INDEX

1. What per cent of the world's population lives in the U.S? (a)—1%, (b)—5%, (c)—10%, (d)—15%, (e)—20%.
2. What per cent of American workers are in law-enforcement jobs? (a)—¼%, (b)—½%, (c)—1%, (d)—2%, (e)—5%.
3. What are your chances of suffering from a serious crime this year? (a)—1 in 100, (b)—2 in 100, (c)—3 in 100, (d)—5 in 100, (e)—10 in 100.
4. What per cent of the victims of crime are under 30 years old? (a)—70%, (b)—55%, (c)—40%, (d)—25%, (e)—10%.
5. What per cent of the victims of crime are black? (a)—70%, (b)—55%, (c)—40%, (d)—25%, (e)—10%.
6. What per cent of married women work at jobs outside the home? (a)—50%, (b)—40%, (c)—30%, (d)—20%, (e)—10%.
7. What per cent of U.S. workers are employed in managerial or professional jobs? (a)—5%, (b)—10%, (c)—15%, (d)—20%, (e)—25%.
8. What per cent of workers have jobs in professional athletics or entertainment? (a)—¼%, (b)—½%, (c)—1%, (d)—2%, (e)—3%.

Answers to Distortion Test: The most correct answer to each of the eight questions is b. For every answer in which you checked an a or c, score 2 points. For every d you selected, score 5 points; for every e score, 10 points. Add up your points. If you've scored 50 points or more, you're suspected of watching too much TV; 30 points or more and you may be in the twilight zone. This test is not a scientific instrument but the results should show some correlation between correct answers and the amount of time spent watching television.

The medium of television has so taken over the country that it has become our *only* mass medium. The numbers of people who read a bestselling book, the subscribers to the most successful magazines, the listeners to even the most powerful radio stations and the readers of the most popular newspapers, the pre-TV film crowds are all statistical gnats when compared to the viewers of a network series canceled for lack of an audience.

As a monopoly medium, television is a powerful means of social control. The central fact of television is that it is a one-way communication system. We have perfected the technology so the few can communicate to the many, but not the means whereby the many can communicate with the few. Such a communication restriction is conducive to the acceptance of pseudo-choice as a substitute for free choice.

The only messages allowed on our only mass medium with any regularity are those that can garner corporate backing. Any corporation with an acceptable message can transmit ideas to thousands or millions of homes. But the average citizen cannot communicate as easily with people in his or her own neighborhood or city. Even with money, a group could not buy air time to proclaim that all aspirin is basically alike or that money can be saved by asking a physician to prescribe drugs generically rather than by brand name. But a drug company can spend millions to tell most of the nation that their brand of aspirin provides a "higher level of pain reliever" in the hopes that enough people will be misled into believing more pain relieVER means more pain reLIEF.

Even though the airwaves legally belong to the people and television stations exist for the prime purpose of serving the public, over 50 percent of their available commercial time is sold to a mere handful of corporations. Clearly the three networks are not means whereby we as a nation can learn about ourselves and each other; they are vertical conduits for large corporations. It is more realistic to consider television in terms of a social control device than as a communication medium.

We have seen earlier in this chapter how the more or less "hidden" messages of programming serve as a sermon for the status quo. In the chapter on advertising we will examine ads in television and other media for their hidden messages and contribution to pseudo-choice. But there is a special relation between television and advertising that needs to be considered here. Commercials are commonly considered the price we must pay to watch "free" programs. But from the viewpoint of those who control TV, the programs exist only to gather crowds to watch the commercials. The stations and networks gather crowds and sell this audience to sponsors at a few cents a head (or rather an eye). If a TV schedule were to reflect accurately this program-as-bait philosophy and the economic realities of the medium, it would look something like this:

7:07	A sexy young female discovers that wearing the proper panty hose produces startling results on passing male strangers.
7:07:30	A housewife learns that she can serve her husband better if she takes a painkiller before he arrives home. She attests to the fact that the drug makes her "more interesting."
7:08–7:16	Since attention span is limited, commercials will now be interrupted for ten minutes to show a story in which a kidnapper is released from prison and murdered. At a key point in the story we will return to commercials.
7:16	A housewife discovers that foul odors in her kitchen can be eliminated by a spray can. This discovery ends her social isolation and restores the bridge club to a state of peace.
7:16:30	A group of actors engage in various exotic and dangerous activities to suggest to men that by drinking the right beer they can somehow share vicariously in such excitement while leading ordinary lives.
7:17	Wide-angle lens, exquisite setting and lighting are used to make a small car look like one costing several thousand dollars more.
7:17:30	Commercials again interrupted by the murder story to re-collect viewers for the next series of ads.

Nielsen ratings are not the life-and-death measurement of the heartbeat of the TV industry—sales figures are. The Nielsen ratings simply measure how many potential customers the bait attracts to the ads. If the commercial time cannot effectively sell panty hose, drugs, beer and cars, no Nielsen rating in the world will help.

Corporate advertisers do exert some control over programming content. The most powerful form of control is indirect. Programs acceptable to the network must be aimed at an audience to whom advertisers want to sell. For this reason older viewers, many of whom watch TV heavily for lack of any realizable alternatives, find little of interest in prime-time television where the big money is spent to attract the 18-35 year olds who are the most consumer minded. Programs on issues of concern to a minority of "only" a few hundred thousand or even a million people rarely make the screens during prime time.

More direct forms of control are rarely made public. In the summer of 1974 no Detroit TV station would show a documentary on the car as the culprit in air pollution. The Detroit "educational" station also blacked out the "Chrome-Plated Nightmare," although it did grant a special screening for General Motors executives.

The prescreening of TV shows by advertisers is not unusual. A group called Stop Immorality on TV queried several TV sponsors about their "moral stance," and the replies shed light on how the nation's largest corporations protect viewers from various evils. A Gillette advertising executive said, "We try to see that our advertising runs in programs which are suitable for general family viewing. Under this policy, we have declined to participate as sponsors in programs such as 'The Smothers Brothers' and 'Laugh-In.' "

Miles Labs' media director commented that Miles will never sponsor "Maude" "until we are clearly convinced that the network intends to make suitable program format changes." Eastman Kodak replied that "In programs we sponsor on a regular basis, we do preview all scripts before the airing of the program. If we find a script is offensive, we will withdraw our commercials from the program."

Sponsors are well aware of the relation between program content and commercial messages. In fact, content is often part of the setting for the commercial, placing the viewer in the proper mood to respond favorably to the sales pitch. One way in which programs promote the desire for consumer goods is to ensure favorable exposure of the "good things." Luxury homes, furnishing, clothes and wealthy life-styles are far more common on TV than in reality. Program directors and writers find such settings more "visual" than real-life living rooms and houses.

Any kind of exposure on TV is a form of advertising. To circumvent time limitations placed on the amount of advertising time available, TV has created the "exposure ad" within normally programming content. The TV quiz show is one way in which dozens of products receive TV exposure outside of paid commercial time. Manufacturers provide the products free and sometimes pay an additional fee in return for the identification made when the item is awarded to a contestant. Many quiz shows can be most accurately described as TV's ingenious discovery of how to run a thirty-minute commercial. A second-by-second timing of a randomly selected quiz show revealed that 40 percent of the thirty minutes was devoted to some form of advertising.

Automakers provide free cars to TV (and movie) series in return for favorable exposure. If possible, the "bad guys" will be cast in a car of a competing brand than the one driven by the good guys. Auto dealers provide free cars so that a particular series will use only one make of car. Mannix used to drive a Chevrolet Camaro while the Mod Squad drove Chryslers. Watch action program credits and car chases to determine if the program has a contract with an auto manufacturer. Attractive shots of a particular make of car driven by the hero are a giveaway, especially if the bad guys giving chase drive a nondescript clunker. Watch for shots not needed in the plot development (the hero pulling up in front of a motel) that give the auto "good identification of the product," as a Chrysler public relations official explains. He goes on to note that "Door handles and windshields don't mean anything. We want exposure that's meaningful, such as the side or the entire car, or the car driving into the camera with the nameplate on the screen." Auto executives monitor early screening of the shows to which they have "donated" cars to make sure the exposure is right. As the same Chrysler executive points out, "If it isn't right they'll point it out to the director or producer. At the next screening, if it isn't better, you may have to reduce the number of vehicles they have."

The New York Times media critic Peter Funt explains that the producers of "Hawaii Five-O" have a deal with United Airlines stating that UA planes will be featured frequently on the show in return for a cash payment. The Hawaii run is one of UA's most profitable and the exposure on "Hawaii Five-O" is considered a form of inexpensive advertising.

Clothing manufacturers and stores receive plugs in return for allowing TV show hosts to wear (read that as "model") their suits. Funt explains in his article that "there is hardly a program on television today that does not have some type of promotional arrangement which provides the show with cash and free goods or services." Sometimes viewers are informed of the arrangements by a hurried announcement over the closing credits, but other times the connections are never articulated.

Liquor ads are banned from TV, but the use of the product in the course of programs flourishes. There is no evidence to suggest that producers or anyone else are paid to slip a drink into the script, but alcohol flows freely on TV. The National Association of Broadcasters' code states that "the use of liquor . . . in program content shall be deemphasized." But the *Christian Science Monitor* carefully studied two months of prime-time programming and found that 80 percent of the shows had scenes involving alcohol and a full 62 percent involved hard liquor.

They found that alcohol was the most often seen beverage in the 249 shows viewed. On CBS, for example, in the 87 shows monitored, alcoholic beverages were seen or mentioned 230 times as compared to 159 times for nonalcoholic beverages. Second place went to coffee, another drug, with 95 mentions. Water was a distant third with only 16 appearances. Not only is alcohol present, it is often shown as a way to relax, as a problem-solver, as an indication of glamour, sophistication or maturity.

So even within the programs viewers learn what cars are glamorous and driven by heroes, which airlines the professionals fly, which clothes store Bill Cullen models for and when to use alcohol to relax. Such hidden content of TV is part of its message, part of its mission to teach.

A Roper poll of a few years ago revealed that although people watch more TV than ever before, they rate the programs as less satisfying than in previous years. The poll showed that people watch more but enjoy it less. The reason for this seemingly illogical finding is that TV programs, like an addictive drug, have a built-in failure to satisfy that provides only enough pleasure to bring viewers back for more.

Television is as efficient a closed system as a factory that burns its waste product for fuel to heat and light the plant. The programs provide a degree of satisfaction but they must not satiate or exhaust the emotions. The viewer must be prepared by the programs for the sale pitch of the ads. Programming helps in a very general way to sell the consumptive life-style necessary if TV advertising is to survive. The types of TV programs are limited, therefore, not by the imagination of scriptwriters nor the demands or desires of the viewers, but by the need to serve as suitable settings for the ads. If viewers believe that TV gives them what they want, they have fallen victim to the misconceptions of pseudo-choice.

The influence of television on humans exposed for years to its electromagnetic ray gun spraying images through a screen onto eyes and brains can be seen symbolically in an experiment conducted by John Nash Ott. Ott read that some doctors suspected long hours in front of the tube caused symptoms of nervousness, fatigue, headaches, loss of sleep and vomiting in certain children. He suspected that some sort of radiation from the tube might be responsible and set out to conduct experiments with plants.

He covered half the picture tube of a color TV set with lead shielding, the kind normally used to block out X rays. The other half he covered with photographic paper able to stop visual and ultraviolet light, but allowing other electromagnetic frequencies to penetrate. Next he placed six pots of bean sprouts in front of each half of the TV screen. A control group of bean plants was placed far away from the TV set.

Three weeks later, both the lead-shielded beans and the control group had grown to a normal height of six inches. But the plants exposed to TV radiation had been distorted and stunted into a vine-type growth. Some of the roots of the videoplants had grown upward out of the soil.

The experiment must be applied to people only on a level of symbol, for the fate of bean sprouts and humans diverge in too many ways to allow for science to make comparisons. But the plants exposed to TV during their time of growth were rootless mutations. One can picture the bean sprouts reaching out with roots to embrace the eerie light of the TV in search of the nourishment that could be provided only by their own soil. And so it is with many humans who live in the medium of TV six or more hours daily seeking some kind of life-giving sustenance that cannot be found on the two-dimensional screen.

Fortunately, plants and people cannot be compared. Unlike the bean sprouts, intelligent viewers have the ability to reach out to that household engineer of pseudo-choice and push the button marked "off."

Chapter 2

Eat, Drink, and Be Wary, for the Food Technologist Cometh

The everyday decision of what to eat shows increasing signs of becoming a pseudo-choice. This is true even though no people in history have had so overwhelming a variety of food from which to choose as do twentieth-century Americans. Pseudo-choice has entered the diet because of the change in food from a totally agricultural product to one that is a result of technology. Each year the percentage of food that reaches American tables unchanged by factory processing decreases. As food becomes increasingly equated with the manufacturing process, the consumer becomes more and more dependent on corporate food providers. And it is the food controllers who have the ability to offer eaters their daily pseudo-choice.

If consumers are habituated to food that can be manufactured only in multimillion-dollar factories and prepared by Ph.D.s in chemistry and food technology, a virtual monopoly of the food supply is possible. Any cook can prepare dozens of breakfast foods

41

from corn (the corn can even be grown in a home garden), but only a sophisticated factory can make pink, sugar-coated, corn toaster tarts ready to eat with a free spaceman inside each foil package.

The change in food source from farm to factory is far from complete but has already reached a seemingly irreversible status. The change is as significant as that in transportation from nature (the horse) to machine (the automobile). Both changes are the result of apparently free choices on the part of consumers, both are corporately controlled and both leave a situation that is accepted as normal yet degrades the quality of life in many ways.

If we can believe the evidence of current trends in the food industry and the prophecies of its leaders, future food will resemble the ultimate both in convenience and pseudo-choice—the food pill. The major obstacle is the engineering of consumer acceptance of what at first appears a rather bleak diet. But the public accepted the idea of being sealed in a metal capsule called an automobile for at least a few years of a lifetime and pay dearly for the dubious privilege.

Most readers will find the idea of a food pill revolting and will firmly resolve never to surrender the sensual joy of eating real food. The food pill, they say, is certainly no more than a science fiction fantasy or a nightmare confined to B-grade movies like *Soylent Green*. But some of these same readers, their appetites no doubt stimulated by such fearful considerations, will put down this book and raid the kitchen for a snack that is little more than a prototype of the food pill cleverly disguised to look like a potato chip, cherry pie or even beef Stroganoff. Future food is not something that will arrive with great fanfare on 1–1–84; it is with us now in embryonic form. Astronauts, passengers on airline dinner flights and snack-food addicts stand as signs of future food-consumption patterns. If you enjoyed your food in 1976, you will certainly love the pseudo-choice menu of 1984.

Although the synthetic food chip available in twelve flavors and sixteen shapes is not yet a supermarket reality (and, hopefully, never will be), there are trends that indicate pseudo-choice in food is increasing. These trends are: (1) the normal situation of eater's alienation, (2) corporate control of various foods and grocery outlets, (3) atrophy of the taste buds and the attraction of synthetic foods and (4) the restaurant as a purveyor of glorified TV dinners.

EATER'S ALIENATION

For all of human history the source of food was very evident. One day's harvesting was next morning's breakfast, and Sunday dinner scratched around the front yard during the week. The battle against hunger united the family unit and consumed the vast majority of each member's time. But the Industrial Revolution took work, education and food-gathering out of the family and placed it into the hands of specialists. Food appeared in stores and was meant to take a minimum of time to prepare and "gather." Today, the normal meal should take as little time as possible to prepare and even less to eat. Exceptions to this norm are reserved for special occasions. The long-term result of this change is a loss of contact with the source of food, a phenomenon we shall call eater's alienation.

The alienated eater accepts food as something that comes from a grocery store rather than a farm. A common assumption is that only a few chemists know what is in all those packages so neatly arranged in supermarket rows and bathed all day in Muzak and fluorescent light. Alienated eaters have only minor problems telling their children where babies come from, but few have mustered the courage (or even see the need) to tell about eating cow meat and pigs. To measure the ascendancy of eater's alienation, try telling a four-year-old he or she is about to have cow meat for supper. The child of past ages not only knew where food originated, he probably helped in the slaughter or harvesting.

Few adults have been inside a food-processing factory and just as few know what is in the cellophane and four-color boxes at the supermarket. The average eater does not know what he or she is eating, how it is made, what it contains or even its long-term effects. With this ignorance of food established, the way is open for corporate control and pseudo-choice. To test your own degree of eater's alienation, see how many food products you can identify from the following list of ingredients. Admittedly this is far from a highly valid test of eater's alienation, but it does serve to illustrate the situation.

YOU ARE WHAT YOU EAT?
A FOOD TEST

Below are ingredient lists for six common foods. Each list is arranged in order of quantity. The first ingredient listed is the one that the food contains the most of, last listed is that ingredient the food contains least of. See how many of the six you can identify.

1. Corn syrup solids, vegetable fat, sodium caseinate, dipotassium phosphate, emulsifier, sodium silico-aluminate, artificial flavor and color.

2. Sugar, gelatin, adinic acid, sodium citrate, fumaric acid, artificial flavor and color.

3. Sugar, bleached flour, shortening with mono- and diglycerides and freshness preserver, dried apples preserved with sulfur dioxide, leavening, corn sugar, soy flour, nonfat dry milk, salt, propylene slycol monoesters, sorbitan and monostearate, spices, polysorbate 60 and artificial coloring.

4. Salt, hydrolized vegetable protein, sugar, autolyzed yeast, beef fat, malto-dextrin, onion, beef extract, celery, caramel, disodium inosinate, disodium guanylate.

5. Corn oil, soybean and cottonseed oils, skim milk, salt, lecithin, monoglyceride, isopropyl citrate (.01 percent), calcium disodium EDTA (.007 percent) added to protect flavor, 3.75 units vitamin A, artificially colored with carotene, artificial flavor.

6. Water, hydrogenated vegetable oil, dextrose, sugar, sodium caseinate, polysorbate 60, sorbitan monostearate, propylene glycol monostearate, glyceryl monostearate, artificial flavor, salt, guar gum, algin, artificial color, propellants: nitrous oxide, chloropentafluoroethene.

Answers to You Are What You Eat? test:
1. Nondairy creamer (or cremer or kremer)
2. Wild raspberry Jell-O
3. Pillsbury applesauce batter cake mix
4. Instant beef-style bouillon
5. Margarine
6. Whipped dessert topping

Eater's alienation leads to consequences far more serious than a mere failure to complete successfully a food ingredients test. Ignorance of what is eaten leads to pseudo-choice susceptibility and possibly to poor nutrition. The U.S. Department of Agriculture's annual survey of family eating habits shows that nearly half the families sampled (and these were not poverty families) had what the USDA calls "inadequate diets." In 1955, the figure was only 15 percent, and in 1965 fully 20 percent had inadequate diets. Inadequate means that the diet contains less than two-thirds of one or more of the needed proteins, minerals and vitamins considered vital by the National Academy of Sciences.

A family shopper who complains about the high cost of meat and produce and who knows little about processed food will often forsake true nutrition for the illusion of convenience and economy. On this shopper's list might be Kool-Aid, a powdered drink mix that sells for $7 a pound; a breakfast powder with nonfat dry milk as the main ingredient for $2 per pound; a stuffing mix with flour as the main ingredient for $1.85 a pound; a "hamburger helper" type food that is basically noodles and shortening for $1.69 a pound; prepopped popcorn for $1.80 per pound and a cooking sauce with the main ingredients of skim milk and water for $4.15 a gallon. When such purchases become a standard part of the family diet, there is little doubt that eater's alienation is at work.

Eater's alienation renders a shopper vulnerable to the magic of food technology. Unfortunately, the magicians are working to duplicate the dream of the ancient alchemists. Instead of turning baser metals into gold, they work to turn simple substances such as air, water and basic foodstuffs into "convenience" foods that can be sold for prices higher than steak or any other unprocessed food. To illustrate the progress of the food technology revolution (or "conspiracy" if you prefer), let us take a brief stroll through a typical supermarket.

As we wander through the aisles squinting at fine print on package labels, we begin to learn some of the favorite ploys of the food manufacturers. Just past the coffee display we find a creation of the alchemists at General Foods. They are selling a small tin of "Cafe Vienna" as a gourmet coffee for $3 per pound. A close look at the ingredients reveals that the delicacy is basically a mixture of nondairy creamer and instant coffee. None of the ingredients sold separately cost anywhere near $3 per pound. General Foods must believe that shoppers are willing to pay dearly to have an assembly line mix the two powders. If the new product succeeds, and first reports are encouraging to GF, pseudo-choice will have again asserted its strength.

Moving quickly to more substantial food, we arrive at the small section devoted to canned chili. There are four brands rather reasonably priced around 60¢–80¢ a pound. But three of the beef chilis with beans brands have water as the main ingredient (one of the favorite magic substances of the food alchemists). Only one of the four brands has beans listed as the main ingredient and only one has more beef than water. Perhaps the three should be called chili soup. At least the shopper still can select chili instead of bean soup with beef after a careful study of the labels.

Our experience with chili suggests a game we can play called the "Tell-It-Like-It-Is, Honesty-in-the-Supermarket Game." The object of the game is to find misnamed food items on the shelves and supply honest names based on the real contents of the package.

Over in the large frozen-food section we score our first points for Polynesian Style Dinner. A careful reading of the contents shows that the main ingredient is rehydrated potato flakes. So we wonder at the eating habits of the Polynesians but rename the dish a "Rehydrated Potato Flake Dinner." Farther down the aisle we score again as a frozen Spinach Soufflé becomes "Skim Milk Soufflé with Spinach." The shopper in the frozen-food section still can choose nutritious and convenient items, but the bulk of display space and advertising dollar goes to the increasing number of highly processed mixtures of questionable value. The value of freezing to preserve nutrition and choice year round is rapidly losing ground to freezing as another tool of the food alchemists used to increase corporate profits and offer only pseudo-choice.

In the meat department we find soybeans posing as bacon, sausage and lunch meat. Since soybeans can be grown about ten times faster than cows and since they are high in protein, their use as a food makes sense. But the food technologists are not content to offer a choice between traditional and expensive sources of protein (meat) and tasteful but inexpensive sources of protein provided by soybean products. Instead, they process the soybeans to imitate meat and vegetable products and sell them for prices only slightly lower than the product being imitated. General Mills combines spun soy protein with oil, dried egg whites, artificial colors and flavors and sells it as Bac*Os for $4 per pound—more than the cost of a good cut of steak. Other food companies use soy protein as a meat substitute to cut costs in the manufacture of pizza rolls or beef Stroganoff and similar frozen foods. The cost saving is passed on to the corporation rather than the consumer who is usually unaware the substitution has been made.

General Mills has already tested a line of simulated meats called Country Cuts as part of the Betty Crocker line of food. The Country Cuts are frozen, precooked chunks of texturized soy protein disguised to look, taste and feel like chicken and ham. Swift and Company is experimenting with a combination of soy and real meat to capture what it estimates to be a $200-million-a-year soy substitute market. Its contribution to pseudo-choice is to offer All American Fun Links—a hot-dog substitute already tested in several small markets.

A further tour of the supermarket confirms the suspicion that the shopper is almost forced to choose among an increasing number of highly processed food combinations and must exert extra effort to purchase simple, natural foods. One sign of the strength of pseudo-choice in food is the current interest in natural or organic foods. The food "revolution" has already progressed to the point where the highly processed, additive-laden food is considered normal. Natural or unprocessed food is the exception available at higher prices only to those with a firm resolve to avoid pseudo-choice.

The only ads for natural foods are the price lists in the daily paper for meat and produce, and these often serve only to discourage the less affluent and to draw shoppers to the store. Once in the store, marketing skills and packaging psychology takes over. The sheer volume of space given to processed as compared to natural food is the most powerful form of persuasion. More space is allocated processed foods because they offer higher potential profits to the grocer. A spokesperson for one of the largest food manufacturers says quite candidly that manufactured food will "totally absorb the food industry's energies in the future." *Food*

Engineering, a prophetically named trade journal, notes "the more additives, the higher the potential profit margin."

But even with the temptation of high profits, food technology does not necessarily lead to pseudo-choice unless it is coupled with the ability to control the food market. Unfortunately, there are signs that our food sources are becoming increasingly controlled by a few large corporations.

CORPORATE CONTROL OF FOOD

Once people have only the vaguest idea of what they are eating, the way is open for the corporate control of food. The alienated eater will not eat what is nutritious but what is presented as most convenient, what is advertised as the most elegant or what is packaged in the most seductive box. And the supplier best able to present such pseudo-choices is not the local farmer but the corporate food company. The thousands of products that line the maze of aisles in the supermarket present much less variety than seems apparent.

In *Market Power and Economic Welfare,* Dr. William Shepherd observes that the average market share of the four leading firms in any given food-product line is 55 percent. In other words, an average of four companies share most of the market for any given food item. This average places the food industry as more monopolistic than the rubber and plastics industry, fabricated metals, textiles and most other industries. According to the FTC's Russell Parker, fifty food-processing companies take in over 60 percent of food-processing profits, and the trend toward concentration is increasing.

In areas such as beer and soft drinks, baby food, canned goods, cereal and meat-packing, three to five large firms already thoroughly dominate the field. Ninety percent of the soup Americans buy is Campbell's, and the company has been able to shape the national concept of what soup is. Ninety percent of our breakfast cereal comes from Kellogg, General Mills, Quaker Oats or General Foods; it is they who have decided that breakfast cereal and sugar are almost inseparable. General Foods sells over 40 percent of the nation's coffee under the brand names of Brim, Max-Pax, Maxim, Maxwell House, Sanka and Yuban. In beer, local breweries numbered in the thousands in the 1930s, but today Anheuser-Busch, Jos. Schlitz, Pabst and Coors account for nearly 55 percent of all beer sales, and the control increases slightly each year. In beer, as in automobiles protection against complete pseudo-choice is offered only by imported brands.

In testimony before the House Subcommittee on Monopolies, Ralph Nader presented data culled from unpublished doctoral studies showing near monopoly control by the four leading producers of baby food (95 percent of all sales), baking powder and yeast (86 percent), instant coffee (81 percent), dessert mixes (86 percent), refrigerated dough (87 percent) and catsup (81 percent). Dr. Shepherd places control by the four leading firms as 50 percent for butter, 85 percent for chocolate, 88 percent for chewing gum, 75 percent for blended and prepared flour and 70 percent for ice cream.

Hiding behind the overchoice of brand names in any supermarket is the fact that fifty corporations effectively control much of the food we eat. Although brand names are household words even to toddlers old enough to watch television, the corporations behind the brands are relatively unknown. Some of the largest food companies and the brands they produce include:

Kraftco Corporation (annual sales of about $3.8 billion)
Stay'n Shape and Temp-Tee dairy products, American cheese, Butter Mints, Cheez Whiz, Chefs Surprise, Cracker Barrel cheese, Golden Caesar salad dressing, Great Beginnings, Koogle peanut butter, Kraft brand barbecue sauce, cake mix, mayonnaise, packaged dinners and salad dressings, Manor House coffee, Miracle margarine and Miracle Whip, Parkay margarine, Philadelphia cream cheese, Roka salad dressing, Velveeta cheese, Toffee candy, Sealtest ice cream and other foods, Breyers ice cream, Checkerboard ice cream and Twin Pop.

Beatrice Foods ($3.3 billion in sales yearly)
Clark bars, Holloway candy, Dannon yogurt, Meadow Gold,

Sanalac, Swiss Miss, Viva yogurt, Burney Brothers bakery, Butter Krust, La Choy, Sexton Foods (suppliers to restaurants and institutions), Samsonite luggage, Eckrich meats, Lowrey meat, Airstream travel trailers, Charmglow gas grills, Miracle White laundry products, Spiegel industries, Taylor ice-cream dispensers ("soft" ice cream) and many other brands.

Ralston Purina Co. (annual sales of about $3.1 billion)
Chex cereals, Chicken of the Sea tuna, RyKrisp, Purina Chow pet foods, Van Camp Sea Foods. Restaurants under the names of Bear's Head, Boat House, The Dock, Hungry Hunter, The Jolly Ox, Stag and Jack-in-the-Box.

General Foods Corporation ($2.8 billion in sales annually)
Awake orange drink, Start, Tang, Birds Eye frozen foods, Cool'n Creamy, Cool Whip, Great Shakes, Iceflow slush, Orange Plus, Thick and Frosty shakes, Burger Chef, Burpee Seeds, Jell-O, Calumet, Certo, D-Zerta, Dream Whip, Minute Rice, Kool-Aid, Good Seasons, Batter'n Bake, Open Pit, Shake'n Bake, Swans Down, Toast'em, Maxwell House coffee, Max-Pax, Maxim, Sanka, Yuban, Post cereals. Log Cabin syrup, Gaines pet foods and Vivianne Woodard cosmetics.

Borden, Inc. (sales of about $2.7 billion yearly)
Aunt Jane's foods, Bama Foods, Calo pet foods, Campfire marshmallows, Colonial sugar, Cracker Jack, Cremora, Eagle brand condensed milk, Flavor House nuts, Kava coffee, Melba Toast, Old London foods, ReaLemon, Wyler foods, Borden dairy products, Rich's cake mix, Mystik tapes, Elmer's glue, Wall-Text wall coverings and many others.

General Mills, Inc. (sales of $2.3 billion annually)
Bac*Os, Betty Crocker products, Bisquick, Breakfast Squares, Buc Wheats, Bugles, Cheerios, Chipos, Cocoa Puffs, Crispy Taters, Fruit Helper, Gold Medal, Hamburger Helper, Kix, Lucky Charms, Pepr-O's, Potato Crisps, Saus-O's, Sugar Jets, Total, Trix, Wheat Chips, Wheaties, Good Mark sausages, Gorton seafoods, Kenner toys, Lionel electric trains and Parker Brothers games, including Monopoly.

Norton Simon, Inc. ($1.4 billion in sales yearly)
Canada Dry beverages, Wink, Hunt's Foods, Reddi-Whip, Wesson oil, Max Factor cosmetics, McCall Publishing Co., Ohio Match Company, Crawford's scotch, John Begg scotch, Johnnie Walker scotch, Old Fitzgerald bourbon, Tanqueray gin, Weller bourbons, Gulf Kist fish, United Can Company and Wampole Laboratories.

CPC International (sales of about $1.3 billion)
Best Foods, Hellmann's mayonnaise, Golden Griddle syrup, Karo syrup, Mazola oil, Niagara starch, Nu Soft, Skippy peanut butter, Thomas frozen foods.

Standard Brands, Inc. ($1.3 billion yearly in sales)
Egg Beaters, Fleischmann's margarine, Chase and Sanborn Coffee, Royal gelatin and pudding, Blue Bonnet margarine, Tender Leaf tea, Baby Ruth candy bars, Butterfinger candies, Planters nuts, Canadian LTD whisky, Fleischmann's gin, Old Medley bourbon, White Tavern gin, B&B liqueur, Benedictine, Lloyd's English gin and a wide variety of other wines and spirits.

Procter & Gamble (sales of $6 billion yearly)
Food items include Big Top and Jif peanut butter, Crisco and Fluffo shortening, Duncan Hines, Pringles and Folgers Coffee. Nonfood items include Biz, Bold, Bonus, Cheer, Comet, Duz, Ivory, Joy, Mr. Clean, Oxydol, Spic and Span, Top Job and Zest soaps. Also Crest, Gleam, Head & Shoulders, Lilt, Prell, Scope, Secret and Sure anti-perspirant.

The advertising of these companies all carries a hidden message. No matter if the ads are for Tang, Pringles, Coffee-mate or Kool-Aid they say "eat manufactured food." Contrary to Alvin Toffler, overchoice is not the problem in supermarkets—at least not to the aware shopper. The problem is a limited range in which choice can be made. The pseudo-choice offered is between the products of one corporation or the nearly identical products from another— General Mills or General Foods, take your choice.

The lowly potato chip offers an interesting case study of the development both of corporate control and pseudo-choice. The state of the potato chip market in the early 1970s was one of healthy competition and numerous local producers. Potato chips remained relatively free of corporate control largely because they have a short shelf life and are too expensive to transport over large distances. But since Americans consume about a billion dollars a year worth of the salty chips, the market was eminently worthy of corporate attention.

In late 1973, Procter & Gamble introduced Pringles as a new kind of potato chip advertised as a great new advance in food and a superior chip. The "newfangled chip" was heavily advertised in print and television. P & G makes Pringles from dehydrated potatotes; adds water, mono- and diglycerides, sodium phosphate, sodium bisulfite, BHA, sugar and vitamin C and salt. The mushlike mixture moves along a conveyer belt and is solidified into "perfectly shaped" potato cookies. The "chips" are neatly stacked in a container strongly resembling a tennis ball can and sold for 70 percent more than ordinary potato chips. P & G sold close to $100 million worth of Pringles in 1973 with distribution to only 60 percent of the country. This already represents 10 percent of the potato chip market. In 1976, other corporate giants were tooling up assembly lines to turn out similar dehydrated potato chips and establish what will most likely be a shared monopoly by 1980.

The success of the corporate pseudo-chip will very likely force many of the local manufacturers of the real potato chips out of business. With Procter & Gamble backing Pringles with national advertising, the smaller companies have little hope to compete effectively. Grocers will find that the new chips take up less valuable shelf space and have a higher profit margin than real chips. Consumers will find that the BHA will keep the chips tasting like instant potatoes for years without spoilage. The potato chip aficionado of the future will be offered a pseudo-choice among various brands of dehydrated chips. Perhaps real potato chips will be offered in the gourmet (or "organic foods") department for $10 a pound.

Even the decision on where to shop is tinged with elements of pseudo-choice. A significant percentage of the time that decision leads to one of three or four of the largest supermarket chains in the nation. Safeway, A & P, Kroger and ACME (American Stores) account for over one-fifth of all grocery sales in the United States in dollar volume. Add to the big four other chains such as Lucky, Jewel, Winn-Dixie, Food Fair, Grand Union and Supermarkets General, and the total jumps to nearly one-third of all food purchases. Twenty corporations own the retail outlets at which 40 percent of all food sales are made.

But the true level of oligopoly control is understated by these figures. A study in 1973 sponsored by the grocery industry and conducted by Metro Market Studies, Inc., found that in many cities the four largest chains (not necessarily the four largest in the country) have a near monopoly on grocery sales. In Akron, Ohio, the big four control 64.5 percent of sales; in Denver, Colorado, 74.3 percent; in Little Rock, Arkansas, 86.1 percent; in Seattle, Washington, 88.2 percent; in Washington, D.C., 71.8 percent. In these cities the food shopper is consistently restricted to a narrow range of choices.

The large food chains are not necessarily the most efficient or the best stores; they simply have the most money muscle. Between 1955-65 the top twenty supermarket chains purchased 272 stores and smaller chains, adding a total of 2600 more outlets and $3 billion in sales to their corporate coffers. The stores bought out were not near failing; rather, they were efficient competitors. The National Commission on Food Marketing, which supplied these statistics, concluded that many of the mergers "probably hurt potential competition."

Pseudo-choice in the decision where to shop has the potential for leading to artificially high food prices and all the other disadvantages of a lack of healthy competition. It also limits the chances for small food producers to obtain sales space in the local supermarkets to increase the shopper's real choice.

In spite of their corporate control, supermarkets have become something of a symbol of American affluence and freedom of choice. The packages of food sit politely on the shelves, no salesperson urges the purchase of this brand or that new product. Each shopper is free to choose from the thousands of options and the selection is unparalleled anywhere else in the world.

In *Future Shock*, Alvin Toffler finds in the supermarket yet another example of overchoice but does see some fault in them:

By wiping out thousands of little "mom and pop" stores they have without doubt contributed to uniformity in the architectural environment. Yet the array of goods they offer the consumer is incomparably more diverse than any corner store could afford to stock. Thus at the very moment that they encourage architectural sameness, they foster gastronomic diversity.

Toffler seems to think that the mom-and-pop stores offered Americans a treasure of architectural delights. In reality, the corner stores were most often dreary affairs with large windows covered with "specials" signs and sun-faded displays. Architectural diversity was set back not a minute by the demise of the mom-and-pop stores.

Mom-and-pop stores were able to offer local specialties and keep food in stock required by the neighborhood. They could offer personalized attention, credit and understanding. What Toffler fails to see is that mom-and-pop stores have not vanished, they have been replaced by corporate parent figures. The Southland Corporation, for example, operates 7-Eleven "convenience" stores, and accounts for nearly 50 percent of all nonsupermarket food sales. The so-called "convenience" stores are nothing more than what the mom-and-pop stores used to be but now controlled from corporate headquarters instead of mom's and pop's back room. Today's convenience stores are built on the model of the modern supermarket rather than the older corner grocery store.

FUTURE FOOD

A decline in food taste and corporate control of the food supply seem to be related. No one has seriously accused Wonder Bread, Hostess Twinkies, Rice Krispies or TV dinners of being overflavored. Corporate control offers eaters a choice among a variety of blandness. Bland food is acceptable because it is now considered normal and atrophy of the sense of taste has set in. Taste bud atrophy need not be a physical process observable under a microscope; it need only be psychological. There is some evidence to suggest that our sense of taste is declining.

Psychologist Dr. Susan Schiffman fed a variety of foods to subjects and asked them to identify the food by taste alone. Sight clues were eliminated by a blindfold and texture clues erased by putting the foods through a blender until they all resembled baby food. In a group of normal-weight subjects only 41 percent were able to identify the taste of bananas correctly. The number jumped to 69 percent for a group of obese people and dropped to 24 percent among elderly people.

Reports in the *Journal of Marketing Research* undertaken to study consumer preference give further hints that taste buds are wearing thin. In a test of over three hundred confirmed beer drinkers, one study found that the prime consideration in taste ratings was the label. Drinking from a six-pack without labels, the beer lovers decided the quality of the beer was not very good and showed no particular preference for one bottle over another—even though their favorite brand was included as one of the unlabeled bottles. Later, given the same six-packs, this time with the proper brand labels, the taste ratings improved measurably and drinkers showed a definite preference for their own brand.

Another study tested forty-two shoppers tasting four loaves of identical bread labeled only as brands L, M, P and H. Each person tried each "brand" and within twelve trials half of those tested settled upon one particular brand preference.

In an experiment at the University of California's Davis Campus, visitors to an open house were given miscolored food. Orange sherbet with green coloring or lime sherbet colored red confused 75 percent of the tasters. The same experimenters found that drinkers could not tell the difference between red wine and white wine colored to look like red wine.

Not only is the discriminating taster becoming the exception, but the standards for judging tastes are changing. The age of pseudo-choice is also the age of imitation imitation. Food technologists at first strove to imitate natural flavors. But eaters have become so accustomed to artificial flavors that they have in turn become the standard by which natural flavors are judged.

The era of imitation imitation is best illustrated by the story of a major food processor who attempted to market a better catsup. The processor spent money for research and finally developed a catsup that preserved the smell and taste of real tomatoes. In spite of a superior product and promotion the tasty catsup flopped. The company had succeeded in eliminating from catsup the taste of overcooked, somewhat scorched tomatoes that is imparted in the normal processing. But it is precisely this overdone flavor that eaters associate with "real catsup." So the company made a few scorching adjustments to alter the catsup's taste and sales again turned profitable.

Charles Grimm, director of flavor creation at International Flavors and Fragrances, Inc., says that "more than ever before manufacturers request the taste of a product as it is usually found in the marketplace—processed, concentrated, freeze-dried, powdered or canned." The processed has become the norm. Food "flavorists" call this phenomenon the pineapple-juice bias. The taste that people associate with pineapple juice is invariably that of an artificial flavor. Part of that artificial flavor is the metallic taste the juice gains from the can, and part is the main ingredient of the pineapple flavoring agent—ethyl butyrate, ethyl acetate and butyric acid. Pineapple juice straight from a pineapple would be rejected as undrinkable, and few would even be able to identify the taste in a blindfold taste test.

Millions of kids raised on powdered orange drinks find real orange juice tastes "funny." Their wrinkled noses mean that the real thing is not sweet enough for palates accustomed to General Foods astronaut powder. There is a children's storybook that has its young readers solve a mystery with clues presented as scratch and sniff papers, or "microfragrances" as 3M calls them. These printed smells are excellent training for children growing up in a world of manufactured food. Each of the smells is genuine imitation imitation. The odor encapsulated to resemble chocolate smells no more like chocolate than the brown-colored coatings used on most ice-cream bars.

It is among children that one can find the signs of future food acceptance. Psychologists who have studied food preferences among adults find that people tend to prefer the food that they become accustomed to as children. An experiment at Miami of Ohio University shows that rats raised on water spiked with garlic later preferred garlic water to plain water. The yearning for food the way Mother used to make it is no mere figure of speech, it is a recognition of a partially conditioned response. If Mother serves cardboard bread and TV dinners regularly, chances are that each bite is an advance toward complete pseudo-choice in the future of food.

Totally synthetic food is so far limited to laboratory experiments and science fiction. The concept of synthetic food is simply one of substituting chemical manufacture for biological processes. This has already happened with rubber, once made only from natural rubber tree plants, and also to fibers for cloth once made only from cotton or other plants. Just as consumers have accepted synthetic fibers in clothing, they seem destined to accept synthetic food as part of the diet of the future.

V. D. Ludington, vice-president of corporate research for General Foods, has said, "We are moving gradually into a world of designed consumer foods. Natural farm produce such as milk, potatoes and grains are no longer just complete foods to be eaten as part of a meal. They have become ever-expanding sources of raw materials to be utilized as building blocks for new and more diverse . . . synthetic foods."

Magnus Pyke, biochemist and president of Britain's Institute of Food Science and Technology, writes, "In all the numerous discussions of different methods of producing food, the possibility of manufacturing it by direct chemical synthesis is commonly overlooked. Yet the scientific knowledge of how this can be done is already available. . . . If science allows us to make the ingredients it is surely not unreasonable to expect that technology will be able to fabricate them in attractive commodities. After all, the motive for doing so is a strong one" (*Synthetic Food* [New York: St. Martin's Press, 1971]).

Paid experimenters have already subsisted for nineteen weeks on a mixture of pure chemical nutrients. If real food becomes either too expensive to produce or insufficient to feed the world, then synthetic food can appear in the attractive role of savior. Synthetic food, like oil, can easily be controlled by a few large corporations who will then hold the power of life and death.

PSEUDO-CHOICE AND THE FROZEN-FOOD MENU

Americans currently eat one out of three meals away from home, and industry analysts expect to see that figure increase to one out of every two meals. The restaurant business is far less monopolistic than the grocery-store or food-processing industries, and any large city offers true choice in eating out. But pseudo-choice is invading even the realm of the dinner menu.

Because of rising costs of food and labor and heavy advertising on the part of the frozen-food industry, restaurant owners are increasingly filling the menu with frozen, precooked, ready-made items from large food processors. Many restaurants do a high-volume business acting as a dispenser of glorified TV dinners. From its status as lifeboat food for a shipwrecked dinner schedule, the frozen meal has moved into gourmet restaurants. Sam Martin, editor of *Quick Frozen Foods* magazine, claims that 80 percent of the better restaurants (not counting fast-food franchises) use some frozen entrées.

Armour Foods sells ready-made entrées such as Coq au Vin, Lumache, Empanadas and Veal Cordon-Bleu to restaurants for as little as 50 cents a serving. How much the restaurant can charge for the frozen dinner depends on the skill of the menu writer and the atrophy of the customer's taste buds. Another company offers frozen steaks with grill marks crisscrossing the bottom so customers will never suspect a microwave oven.

That restaurants serve frozen food does not in itself contribute to pseudo-choice, nor does it inevitably lead to poor taste or nutrition. But to the extent that restaurants become dependent on preprocessed, ready-to-serve foods, they become dependent on the leading processors. The question to ask a waiter is no longer who is your chef but do you order from General Mills, Sara Lee or Armour?

Another temptation to restaurant owners is to substitute less expensive food for the real thing. Thanks to the food alchemists and taste-bud atrophy, many restaurants serve one kind of food masquerading as another. For example, that cherry garnishing the cottage cheese salad or ice-cream sundae might not be a cherry at all. Tri-Valley Growers of San Francisco markets a product called

"Grapes Jubilee." The Thompson grapes are colored to look like cherries yet cost far less than maraschinos. General Mills offers a product called Protein II, a textured vegetable protein with artificial ham flavor. Protein II is sold to restaurants to replace ham in ham and eggs. According to the General Mills ad, "These chewy crumbles of textured vegetable protein are a convenience and economical replacement, and very likely most people won't realize that they're not eating 'the real thing.' "

Bontrae Protein Products offers textured vegetable protein disguised as tuna and intended to be mixed with real tuna to stretch both the tuna and profits. Anderson Clayton Foods offers a product called "Unique Loaf" that looks and tastes like natural cheese but is made from protein and vegetable oils. Their ads urge, "Replace your natural cheese requirements with Unique Loaf and give your recipes all the flavor and appearance of real cheese at a fraction of the cost." Other common extenders use vegetable protein to imitate tomato sauce, eggs and gravy.

Some restaurants offer Roquefort cheese salad dressing on the menu but serve blue cheese dressing instead, knowing that few people will notice the difference. The same kind of lower-priced substitution takes place in fish dishes. Roy Martin, director of science and technology for the National Fisheries Institute, says that what a fish is named on the box or menu is far more important than how it tastes. Few people can distinguish among the various kinds of fish. The Blue Water seafoods company (which calls itself the "Newfood" people) sells to restaurants and institutions South Atlantic whiting and Alaskan pollack that has been "saberized." Saberizing cuts the gray streaks out of the pollack and the fat layer out of whiting so that the fish looks like cod. The prices are 10 to 20 percent less than cod, and a quite convincing picture in Blue Water's ads shows that only a trained eye could tell the difference between saberized pollack and cod. Since few people would order Alaskan pollack, a restaurant could serve pollack at cod prices and feel safe that eaters will not demand their money back because the fish doesn't taste like cod. Restaurants can deceive eaters only because there are no truth-in-menu laws and because taste buds are so easily misled by packaging and advertising.

CONCLUSION

Pseudo-choice in food will be complete when shoppers and restaurant customers cease to choose from knowledge and instead succumb to the lures of marketing and advertising. It is still possible to purchase simple, nutritious food at fair prices and it is possible to dine where the food is carefully prepared and consistently fresh.

Knowledge of food ingredients, especially of "new foods" offered by the leading food producers, can help the shopper avoid pseudo-food. Books such as Michael Jacobson's *The Eater's Digest*, William Robbins' *The American Food Scandal*, James Hightower's *Eat Your Heart Out* and Beatrice Trum Hunter's *Consumer Beware!* can help immensely in shaping pseudo-choice resistance. Food co-ops help counter pseudo-choice and corporate control of grocery outlets as does participation in growing or raising one's own food supply. Convenience foods certainly have some place in the eating hierarchy, but one reserved for those emergencies when time is of the essence.

Home economics or consumer education teachers should make students aware of the corporate control of the food supply as well as the nature of the most common processing ingredients. The nature and uses of food would seem to be high on the list of important knowledge for both personal and social survival. School cafeterias and lunchrooms with vending machines often counteract any classroom teaching by serving pseudo-food delights and dispensing only sweets and soft drinks for snacks.

If the best food as we know it today does not exist for the citizen of the future, it will be because of the victory of pseudo-choice. Just as with automobiles and television, we will be offered a pseudo-choice and will pretend it is an expression of free will and a monument to our freedom as a nation.

Chapter 3

The Mechanical Centaur:
To Drive or Not to Drive,
That Is the Pseudo-Choice

*A tourist came in from Orbitville,
parked in the air, and said:*

*The creatures of this star
are made of metal and glass.*

*Through the transparent parts
you can see their guts.*

*Their feet are round and roll
on diagrams or long*

*measuring tapes, dark
with white lines.*

*They have four eyes.
The two in back are red. . . .*

*They all hiss as they glide,
like inches, down the marked*

tapes. Those soft shapes,
shadowy inside

the hard bodies–are they
their guts or their brains?

"Southbound on the Freeway"
—May Swenson, 1936

Those "soft shapes, shadowy inside"—are they the drivers or the driven? And those creatures of metal and glass, are they merely extensions of the human foot or of the owner's inner being?

Almost all writing about automobiles has been about the shells or the drivers. But cars by themselves do not cause problems and rarely are the traffic jams caused by autoless drivers. What must be considered is the symbiotic relationship between auto and driver. For when a human and an auto merge, a new creature is created. We are dealing with a cyborg, half man and half machine, a technological centaur. Let's call this twentieth-century creation Automan—here he comes now.

Automan is crawling through the city at 8 mph, his average downtown speed. He believes there are hundreds of horses pulling him and knows this is true by the shiny chrome number fastened on the side of his shell. He likes the organic, wild West feel of the word "horsepower." He is a wheeled package of steel, glass and plastic sometimes controlled by a logical brain, sometimes by unpredictable impulse.

This Automan represents the coming together of two trends— humans becoming more machine-like and machines becoming more human. Where the two meet is a biogenic machine or a mechanized human. Machines will never rise up and kick people off the planet, robots will not fight the Second American Revolution nor will computers play chess with nations as pawns. But the machines that can control human life, change life-styles and bring both joy and tragedy have arrived. The machines rolled out quietly and benevolently over the years from Detroit and a few other cities at the rate of one every three and one-half seconds. Since they have no human "weaknesses," such as morality or a concern for human life, they tend to seize control. Supposedly prophetic science fiction writers picture gargantuan monsters from the sea or nightmare creatures from outer space taking over the cities. But they lost their prophetic nerve and failed to see the dangers of the mechanical centaur who dwells among us one hundred million strong.

The question remains: which is the inhabitant of this third planet from the sun and which its servant? "Those soft shapes, shadowy inside the hard bodies—are they their guts or their brains?" Are the things we call cars evolved from a series of free choices or are they living models of pseudo-choice?

$HELLING OUT

Americans spend one out of every $5 to $6 they earn on automobiles. One out of every six jobs in the nation is devoted to serving the needs of autos and twelve of the *Fortune* top-twenty corporations either make autos or the fuel they consume. There is one auto for every 2.6 humans in the country. The entire nation could sit more or less comfortably in the front seats of all the cars. And at the rate the auto is consuming land, front-seat real estate might become the most practical and affordable. Our urban defenses and suburban fences have proved as effective as the Maginot Line. In Los Angeles and Atlanta more urban land is reserved for autos than for all other uses put together.

Each Automan extrudes fifteen hundred pounds of pollutants into the air each year, costing at least $16 billion measured in purely economic costs. The Automan has no qualms about using chemical warfare. In Chicago, ozone warnings and alerts are so common in the summer months that they are regarded with as much concern as the monthly air raid siren test. Los Angeles honored Automan in the early 1970s by lining Jefferson Boulevard with auto-resistant plastic plants that supposedly thrive on carbon monoxide and other pollutants.

Even back in the 1930s Charles Kettering of General Motors wrote in some now defunct magazine, "Think of the results to the industrial world of putting upon the market a product that doubles the malleable iron consumption, triples the plate glass production, and quadruples the use of rubber. No other artifact in history has affected so many people and so many industries." The auto industry today, according to former General Motors chairman James Roche, uses 61 percent of all rubber consumed in the United States, 20 percent of all steel, 10 percent of all aluminum and one-third of all the glass used in the country.

If Americans would for some reason denounce the auto and change to walking and bicycles, the country would be thrown into economic turmoil. But Americans continue to spend $140 billion or more a year for cars. Yet the cars they spend seven to eight working hours of wages a week to support do not represent the highest state of American technology. Instead autos exemplify the debilitating effects of monopoly capitalism and the economic reality of "dynamic obsolescence."

Within the current state of technology, a car with the following specifications could be built and profitably sold:

Life Span:	200,000–500,000 miles or more.
Safety:	Able to protect most passengers from fatal injuries upon impact with a brick wall at 60 mph.
Economy:	25 to 50 miles on 1 gallon of fuel. Little maintenance and easy repairability.
Comfort:	Smooth quiet ride.
Cost:	No more than current prices.

The reason such a car does not exist has more to do with economics than technology. Alvin Toffler in *Future Shock* becomes nearly ecstatic at the freedom of choice mass production provides the consumer. Using the Mustang as an example, he claims that to make a wise selection of options on a new model might require days of reading and research. What he neglects is that the choices presented to the consumer are of superficial matters such as plastic that looks like wood or plastic that looks like plastic, $30 for a white stripe around the tires or no white stripes, various strips of chrome, or engines that manage either nine or fourteen miles per gallon. The choices include none that would result in a car such as described above. The options presented are pseudo-choices designed to provide a taste of freedom.

In spite of huge budgets for research and development, the auto in the United States has improved far less than it could have since the Model T. Cars today are more reliable but they have tended toward complexity of operation rather than simplicity. The more moving parts in a machine the greater the likelihood of a breakdown. Detroit's improvements have made the car so complex that few can repair or understand it when it does inevitably break down. A biased but strong case can be made for the fact that the Model T was in many ways better than today's cars.

None of the recent major improvements in automobiles came from the United States—disc brakes, fuel injection, hydropneumatic suspension, the rotating piston, torsion bars, split axles, fluid drive, direct drive shafts—all were borrowed from European inventors.

The first auto was put together more or less by chance by a Frenchman, Emile Levassor, back in 1895 when he placed an engine instead of a horse in front of his wagon. The engine Levassor used was a German invention, ridiculously inefficient, requiring the piston to go up and down three times before anything really happened. Of course, we still use the internal-combustion engine today, a feat similar in technological wisdom to using a sewing machine motor to power an airplane or coal to run a locomotive.

To Detroit, automobile improvements mean making cars more salable, rather than more efficient or functional. An increase in gas prices, environmental protection agency actions or a real or imagined gas shortage produce only token improvements in efficiency. Money is spent to produce material which is a cheaper substitute for some item already used—the amount of plastic in cars is steadily increasing. Most of the minor improvements announced in new models can be found in other cars made twenty or thirty years earlier.

But what of ecology and safety pressure groups forcing Detroit to make cars safer and cleaner? Ralph Nader and friends have indeed caused some worries but their most notable achievement so far is that they have helped convince the public that they should spend $300 to $700 more per car to keep down air pollution. Controlling pollution in an internal-combustion engine is similar to building a tower to put a beacon light on so that airplanes don't crash into the tower and then heralding the tower as a lifesaver. This image of the tower built to hold a light to warn planes away from the tower is similar to the kind of thinking that governs much of Automan's behavior and his relations to society.

THE DIALOGUE OF THE OPEN ROAD

Automobiles are not mere transportation machines. They are a mass medium used by drivers to broadcast the state of their ego, opinions about the world and their feelings about the guy next door. The most obvious indication of the auto as mass medium is the commonly accepted use of bumper stickers.

Similar stickers placed on house windows or on placards on front lawns are virtually nonexistent. Even message buttons are rare outside of election time. But bumper stickers are alive on every freeway and carrying on their daily cacophony of Day-Glo clichés ranging from "Honk if you're horny" to "We visited a snake farm."

Why should the common people choose the automobile to carry the weight of the right to free speech or the need to philosophize? The automobile as a mode of expression is one of the few channels open to the ordinary person to reach the masses. Television, radio and newspapers are open only to hired professionals or businesses with thousands of dollars to buy time or space—a bumper sticker still costs only $1 and reaches thousands. The popularity of citizen band radio should surprise no one—CB is an electronic bumper sticker.

But even more crucial a reason for the auto doubling as a soapbox on wheels is the fact that the auto and the driver are a unit—the mechanical centaur rides again. The owner of an auto to some extent identifies with the car as an extension of the self. This identification is what makes the car an ideal vehicle to serve as the ordinary person's editorial page. What the car "says" is what *I* say, believes Automan. And this is true not only for bumper stickers, but also for the nonverbal messages each car sends to the world of the open road.

Even children have learned to identify with cars. Ask a child to draw a picture of a car and the results could very well be a revealing self-portrait. University of Iowa psychologist Jan Loney has devised a "Draw-A-Car" test that begins with a drawing and continues as the child plays the role of a car salesman and the therapist a prospective buyer. The child is less defensive in talking about the rusts or dents of a car than his own hidden faults. Loney has found the test is especially effective for bed wetters and children who defecate involuntarily. He speculates that the test is effective because both cars and people have nutritional and eliminative systems. A child unable to control himself or herself might say about his or her car, "It's got bad brakes." A superconformist might say the car holds the road real good.

Instead of taking long and tedious case histories, therapists for Automen might ask a patient to talk about the cars he or she has owned or bought.

"You are what you drive" claims a sports car ad, but more likely a correct statement would be, "You drive what you would like to be." A car is for many people like Clark Kent's underwear—it turns the mild-mannered citizen into a superman, able to control hundreds of horses with a single button, able to move faster than a bankrupt locomotive or even leap tall mountains with barely a shudder. A car does not merely "run"; it "means," "expresses" and "reveals."

When Automan decides to buy a new shell, his inner needs and desires confront the psycho sell of Detroit. Auto showrooms and ads no longer offer mere Fords or Chevys; instead they sell a veritable bestiary of mythical creatures. There are cougars, pintos and mustangs, star fires and thunderbirds to offer years of study to a scholar of Modern American Mythology.

Henry Ford's "Model A" and "Model T" were good cars with practical, easy-to-learn-and-remember names. But they held no wondrous promises and met no secret desires. Today, Ford's heirs have learned (with the occasional exception of an unimaginative choice like Edsel) the importance of a name. People speak less and less about General Motors, Chrysler or even Chevrolet and Ford. Instead they commonly use the name given to a car from a combination of creative brainstorming, motivational research and a computer search. Since words shape perceptions, what we "see" out there on the road are the beasts and mythical beings of the imagination.

Professor Robert Heilman, writing in *The American Scholar*, describes automobile names as ". . . subliminal entrapments of our secret selves, betrayers of ambition, limitacy, libody." These subliminal entrapments promise the magic, power and excitement missing from ordinary lives. But what is the effect of these names on the driver once the car is purchased? Does a driver who is taming a Wildcat or Cougar or piloting a Fury or a Tempest or racing at the Grand Prix or Le Mans behave differently from a driver simply guiding a "Model A" or a "Chevrolet"? Would the Automan symbiosis "behave any differently named 'Pacifica' or 'Turtle' or 'Standard'?"

What effect on drivers does the stick-it-to-the-other-guy category of names have? In this category are such aggressive and sharply painful names as Javelin, Matador, Sting Ray, Hornet, Cutlass and Le Sabre. Do the people who purchase cars in this group have a sublimated desire to "stick" others?

And what of the names that promise power unlimited? Names like Coronet, Marquis, Squire, Ambassador and Imperial connote royalty and high standing. Culture critic Arthur Asa Berger points out in *Pop Culture* that ". . . there may be an inverse correlation between a person's sense of 'self' and the size of the engine of his car. People who feel petty and insignificant, for whatever reason, may need gigantic V-8's, and people who feel weak may need 'muscle' cars."

And the animals that roam our roads speak of a kind of ancient animism, a desire to recapture the worshiped attributes of wild animals.

Would a complete change in auto names result in less aggressive driving?

Upward Bound Names	Exotic and Usually Upper-Class-Places	Speed Names
Landaus	Calais	Bonneville
Broughams	Newport	Le Mans
Regal	Capri	Grand Prix
Coronet	Riviera	Mercury
Marquis	Monterey	Comet
Squire	Malibu	Mach I
Continental	Catalina	Monza
Imperial	Monte Carlo	
Ambassador	El Dorado	
LTD	Monaco	
	Aspen	
	Cordoba	

Power Names	Animal Names	Stick-it-to-the-Other Guy Names
Charger	Colt	Javelin
Fury	Mustang	Matador
Tempest	Hornet	Sting Ray
Toronado	Cougar	Hornet
Cyclone	Jaguar	Cutlass
Triumph	Manta	Le Sabre
Galaxy	Sting Ray	Arrow
Nova	Pinto	
Demon	Falcon	
Starfire	Safari	
Impala	Sky Hawk	
	Firebird	

Auto animism uses only the names of those animals the city-bound dweller imagines as being "wild" and "free." There are no cars named Cheshire or Beagle or Canary, no matter how lovable or desirable these creatures might be. The animal names used for cars are those that connote freedom and rapid movement. And these two qualities are very much a part of auto psychology.

An 1889 Stanley Steamer ad struck the chord resonantly when it proclaimed, "The delight which comes of rapid movement has never been understood until one occupies a place in a horseless carriage on a smooth road. There is an exhilaration from the swift motion surpassing that of any other form of movement." The sensation of speed is perhaps the twentieth century's only unique contribution to the catalog of widely enjoyed human pleasures.

The automobile fills the human "need" (or "desire"—to avoid academic controversy) for movement. In his book, *The Natural Mind*, Andrew Weil writes of the innate need to "get high." He points out that children seek out dizziness and rapid movement and that various carnival rides offer a kind of altered consciousness. The comparison between the need for drugs and the need for the auto is not without grounds. Part of the auto's appeal is that of movement. Car driving is something done for its own sake, as a kind of movement therapy, perhaps for some of the same reasons that people use drugs.

Not only has the auto helped satisfy this craving for the experience of moving (as distinct from moving for the sake of getting from one place to another), it has changed the very nature of that experience.

At the Museum of Science and Industry in Chicago, there is an operating model of a coal mine. The tour includes an elevator ride down the mine shaft and a ride on a trolley car through the dark mine tunnel. I went through the mine at age seven or so and was amazed that the museum had a coal mine for a basement. Many years later I went back and realized that the whole mine is an illusion, nothing more than a basement museum room. The elevator moves a bit as does the trolley car, but the illusion of movement is created by a moving wall. The trolley car rocks, wind is blown past the riders and few realize they have moved only a few feet. I have been unable to convince others who have taken the tour that the ride was not "real."

The mine simulation points up the relativity of motion. We can experience motion either as moving in relation to stationary objects or as stationary objects moving in relation to self. In the automobile the experience of movement is similar to that of the coal mine. In a tightly closed auto we watch as the outside moves by us; the "experience" of motion is nearly missing on smooth roads and soft rides. Travel becomes more like watching a movie than experiencing movement. The automobile serves as a filter between those inside and the environment—it becomes its own environment.

The educational and cultural enrichment of travel can no longer be measured by the number of miles covered. The auto traveler sees only the road and large landmarks or areas marked "scenic" or "historical area." The wildlife, the planes, the terrain, even the special quality of the air often go unnoted by Automan. Superhighways and new cars limit the experience of movement, but they also supply a limited feeling of freedom.

Some people call the open road a "freeway"; engineers label the same road a limited-access highway. Both terms contain a kernel of philosophy. The interstate highway system is a source and symbol of freedom. Those who travel the system experience a kind of isolation therapy in which they can enjoy a freedom from the telephone, interruptions and all demands other than staying between the white lines.

As the auto (and the airplane) remove the experience of movement, people search elsewhere for the rush and thrill of speed. Motorbikes, bicycles, snowmobiles and sports cars are used to restore the sense and thrill of movement to travel.

Americans very much equate movement with freedom. To be free means to be able to move anywhere at any time. Criminals and bad children alike are punished by physical barriers to mobility. Just as the auto provides an illusory experience of movement it also satisfies the need for the illusion of freedom.

When people speak of "freedom," they mean not so much the human demand as the *feeling of* freedom. Erich Fromm in *Escape from Freedom* clarifies the point that real freedom is a painful and heavy burden that few seek to carry. What is sought is a negative freedom, a freedom from, an absence of control. The automobile provides a heady illusion of freedom, turning an ordinary mortal into superman for a few hours, shutting out problems and providing an inviting array of thousands of miles of random-access roads. But the automobile demands a heavy price for the pseudo-choice of freedom.

The promise of free choice is first held out in the auto showroom. It is here we meet Herman, an ordinary man in the process of shedding his Automan skin. Hundreds of options allow Herman to exercise his freedom of choice. Of course, no matter what his choice the car will very likely be manufactured by one of the three large auto manufacturers. And, as noted earlier, his choices do not include those that would make his car safe, economical or reliable. The first price to pay for this "free choice" is the price on the car which translates as perhaps from five hundred to one thousand hours of hard work. Now that the $4000 technological dodo filled with mechanical bugs is purchased, Herman heads home to Plum Valley, a suburb twenty-five miles from city center where he works.

On his way home he doesn't really consider that he was forced to buy a car because there is no practical public transportation and nothing within walking distance of his mini-"estate." To view the purchase of an auto as a forced decision would be to destroy the illusion of freedom. The fact that Herman will spend about forty days a year or one and a half years of his work life belted inside his

metal capsule does not disturb him—this is part of the price he
must pay to get away from the city. All that traffic in the city
makes raising children on the streets too dangerous.

In reality Herman has chosen from among a highly limited
number of choices. He is economically enslaved to his auto and its
support and a prisoner of its jealous demands on his time. He pays
taxes that are, in effect, a subsidy of the auto as *the accepted means* of
transportation. The automobile is a simulation of totalitarian rule.
It benevolently holds out the promise of freedom while offering
pseudo-choice in disguise.

Alexis de Tocqueville wrote of totalitarian rule as one that ". . .
every day renders the exercise of the free agency of a man less
useful and less frequent . . . Such a power does not destroy, but it
prevents existence . . . it compresses, enervates, extinguishes and
stupefies people." His statement fits the Automan empire nicely.
As Herman heads home in his new alter ego, he enjoys the illusion
of freedom. After all, isn't that why the road is called a freeway?

But Herman's feeling will soon be tempered by creeping dissatisfaction. Herman will be taught that this feeling of discontent is
really a desire to get ahead or expand his freedom by buying a
bigger or more luxurious car. His disappointment will reach a peak
when the new models are brought out. The reason for this precise
timing is that Detroit's advertising orchestrates the feelings of Automan.

Many years ago General Motors' Alfred Sloan explained why
the auto industry brings out a new model every year. He explained
with exceptional candor that, "We want to make you dissatisfied
with your current car so you will buy a new one, you who can
afford it." So auto advertising is designed to frustrate and make the
owner dissatisfied. The ad campaigns attempt as much to unsell
you on your current car as they do to sell you a new one. This
insight helps explain why auto ads depend so much on psycho sell
and fantasy images instead of solid and useful consumer information. The various auto ads don't compete with each other as much
as they cooperate to maintain the desirability of frequent auto
purchases.

Herman does not know that he pays for his own feelings of
inferiority in his own Automan skin to the tune of $30 to 70 per car

for advertising. He also does not know the tremendous cost of yearly model changes that he helps promote by buying a car every year or two.

In the May, 1962, issue of the *American Economic Review* a team of three economists reviewed, "The Costs of Automobile Model Changes Since 1949." They set out to find out how much less an auto would cost if annual model changes were eliminated and autos changed only when new technology invited real improvements in performance or safety. Their calculations showed that about $700 per car (25 percent of purchase price in 1960 dollars) or about $3.9 billion per year between 1956-60 was the cost of what GM calls "dynamic obsolescence." The style changes enable the auto manufacturers to provide the illusion of progress and entice a greater consumption of new product. The one-half billion dollars spent yearly on advertising for autos is thus not a luxury but essential in perpetrating the illusion of progress.

THE AUTOMAN EMPIRE

Civilization is adapting itself to the automobile, not the automobile to civilization. The auto affects each of us personally to the extent we allow it, but its strongest influence is on the social and physical environment we have built to suit the car. Whether we drive or not, whether we are a car buff or a dues-paying member of the Concrete Opposition, we live in an environment shaped by the automobile.

The Automan Empire is paved with good intentions of politicians and taxpayers' money, not to mention enough asphalt to cover all of New England. Part of the problem with our road system is that it is so good. We experience the joy of speeding along a limited-access freeway at a mile a minute with few problems. A traffic jam is a great tragedy—it is a fall from higher expectations. Traffic and rush hour are almost interchangeable in the thought of Automan, for it is here that the system is the most vulnerable.

Fifteen billion dollars yearly are spent building roads at the rate of two hundred miles a day (for the past twenty years), which nearly equals the money spent educating our nation's teenagers.

Many roads still follow Indian trails, historical quirks or political gerrymandering. The city streets in San Antonio are built along cattle trails and only Washington, D.C., has method to its traffic madness, obsolete as it may be.

Every time Automan gulps a gallon of gas as much as 30 percent of the purchase price is used to buy concrete for a new or "improved" road. The money goes into a special Highway Trust Fund which is used to build roads. The financing is a self-perpetuating system which assures that transportation efficiency will be secondary to road building. The arrangement is similar to using the tax from alcohol to strengthen the liquor industry.

The money from the fund is given to states on a 90-10 arrangement; the city or state government puts up 10 cents and the government matches it with 90 cents. The 10 cents dollar is a politician's dream, far better than any other dollar for health, education or welfare.

In 1956 the Federal Highway Act started the tires rolling for the Interstate System. The mood of the fifties enabled the Interstate System to capitalize on the red scare and claim to be a defense system needed in case of attack. Many bridges built in the fifties had clearances designed to accommodate the tallest weapon the army had at the time that could be transported by truck.

The Interstate System was to be for intercity travel only, but local governments couldn't resist the 10-cent dollar and so today the red, white, and blue signs often mark city expressways built for as much as $50 million per mile. The Interstate has been subject to cost overruns that would make the military feel at home. Currently the great highway machine has paved an area equal to nearly 400 square miles, and used enough sand, gravel and stone to build a wall around the world fifteen feet wide and nine feet high. The same government statistics show that the Interstate System has used enough concrete to build six sidewalks to the moon and lumber from all the trees in a 400-square-mile forest. Now if only the Highway Fund could be converted into a Transportation Fund.

The relation between roads and autos is mutually parasitic. As Henry Ford himself foresaw: "For every good road built, more automobiles will be used, and with the use of every automobile the demand for more good roads increases." The vicious (or "magic" if you're in the right business) circle goes something like this: roads encourage travel, more travel sells more gas, more gas yields more tax, more tax builds more roads, more roads encourage more travel, etc., etc., etc.

There is a variation of Parkinson's Law which applies to transportation: it states simply that the number of autos increases to fill the available space. This means that the cry for more roads is totally ineffective as is the cry for more garage space in urban areas. Both roads and automobile storage space do not alleviate congestion, they generate more traffic.

A more exact and carefully researched "law," Downs's Law, states that "on urban commuter expressways, peak-hour traffic congestion rises to meet maximum capacity." Realizing this, even auto and oil industry executives are now speaking in favor of mass transit. They view mass transit not as an alternate means of travel but as a device to protect the auto at its most vulnerable point—rush hour.

Automan has a way of proposing to solve the very problems it creates. First the auto contributes heavily to congestion and urban deterioration. Then it provides the means for people to escape the congestion of the city by making suburbs possible. This in turn causes the city to lose tax revenue because it must build more roads. The auto and related forces are now well on the way to destroying suburbs. Each cycle of problem and solution pushes the auto onto a new frontier and renders it even more essential to urban survival. In the process of solving problems the auto has helped to alienate humans from nature and from contact with others.

The automobile permits only limited personal interactions, most often of an aggressive, competitive nature. Social scientist Edward Hall writes in *The Hidden Dimension* that "If people are to be brought together again, given a chance to get acquainted with each other and involved in nature, some fundamental solutions must be found to the problems posed by the automobile." Philip Slater, in *The Pursuit of Loneliness*, charges the auto ". . . did more than anything else to destroy community life in America. It segmented the various parts of the community and scattered them so that they became unfamiliar with one another."

The segmented "community" of the city became the place where to be a stranger was the norm and where anonymity was a blessing rather than a curse. But such an environment was no place for children and not much better for adults. So the city dwellers used the auto to leave; they created suburbs in a rare Utopian spirit. But since the automobile also went to the suburbs, the roads became crowded. Because the roads became crowded, more were built, thus destroying more communities and creating further congestion.

Now some of the children of the suburban Utopias are fleeing suburbia much as their parents did the cities. They pile into VWs (originally Hitler's answer to mobilizing the Germans) and set out with grand ideals for new kinds of suburbs called communes. But those autos are still there, just in case a quick escape is needed.

Meanwhile, back in the city, the auto has helped turn downtown areas into solid masses measurable only by cubic feet. A time-lapse film of Chicago's skyline over the past fifteen years would show that it is rapidly becoming one huge cube. Such city cubes will contain places of business but will be almost totally unpopulated. As city planner Victor Gruen put it in *The Heart of Our Cities*, "We turned our cities into doughnuts with all the dough around the center and nothing in the middle."

"ACCIDENTS"

It is amazing that only fifty thousand people yearly are killed in auto accidents. It is even more amazing that the risks of driving are accepted as part of living in an auto-oriented society.

The labels and categories a society uses shape the thinking and action of its members. A commonly used label is prescriptive as well as descriptive. For example, the category of "teenager" is far from neutral. Categorizing a person by the number of times the earth has traveled around the sun (age) is one of thousands of possible classifications. The choice of this one and the consequent elimination of others shape our thinking about the person so labeled.

The use of the word "accident" to describe collision between two autos or between an auto and another object is likewise significant. "Accident" implies that what happened was not done "on purpose." It also tends to imply that the cause of the event was an individual who made some mistake or that such events are not expected. "Accidents" are commonly thought of being "caused" by speeding, failing to stay awake while driving, drinking or simply losing control. If a society believes that these individual actions cause accidents, it will react by passing laws, and giving constant warnings and admonitions to "be careful." That same society will find that these warnings have little effect and so the only recourse is to become angry with the accident-prone driver and to class him or her as criminal. Although no exact statistics are available, it is quite probable that a higher percentage of cars than guns come off the assembly line to injure and kill humans. The fact that an "accident" is unexpected for the individual hides the fact that 25 to 40 percent of all cars injure people in accidents.

In reality, most accidents are not accidental at all. Blaming traffic fatalities on "accidents" is similar to blaming a disaster on the gods or the Fates. Every "accident" is a direct result of the values of society. Take the case of a drunken driver who collides head-on with another auto, killing three people. It is no accident that he was able to drive on the wrong side of the road; it is rather an expression of the fact that we are willing to take the risk of head-on collisions rather than pay for the barriers to prevent them. It is not accidental that the people were not well-protected in the other automobile since they were unable to purchase a car that would protect them. It is not an accident that the man was drinking or that he was able to enter the traffic system in such a condition. It is not an accident that he very likely had no alternative to a self-propelled vehicle. It is not an accident that he was driving an automobile nor that he was able to travel at a killing speed.

To choose to call transportation failures "accidents" is to risk never eliminating their root causes and to absolve the truly guilty. This same mentality carries into other areas that Charles Reich in *The Greening of America* has identified with Consciousness I. He says: "If a given number of automobiles are crowded onto a highway, there will be a predictable number of accidents. The moral approach tries to deal with this as a question of individual driver responsibility. It stresses safe driving and criminal penalties. Yet reduction of the accident rate is demonstrably a problem in engineering." Public-service ads urge the populace to drive safely, look both ways, etc. But little pressure is put on manufacturers to engineer a more effective people-transporting system.

Most accidents are direct results of engineering and financial decisions. They develop from a series of pseudo-choices. Others are caused by individuals using the auto to commit conscious or unconscious suicide. Many Automen who lose control for no apparent reason are driven by inner fears that cause them to change their destiny in a microsecond when death seems more secure than life on the road.

JUNKYARDS

Every two to four years Automan sheds his metal skin in burial grounds called junkyards. More recently third- and fourth-hand owners simply "do it in the road," leaving the hulks to be pulled away by police or desecrated by the night people.

Junkyards have received a bad press lately as ugly places that pollute the countryside. Perhaps it is our print bias that enables us to see libraries, classified collections of mental junk, as valuable community assets and judge collections of material resources as nuisances to be fenced in and guarded by dogs.

Junkyards are valuable collections of resources that we haven't gotten around to using yet. Junk is misplaced wealth.

When and if the deschooled society ever arrives, the junkyard will be one of the most popular and educational places for the young. Each junkyard would have an educational director skilled in technology, science and history. Perhaps a few of the nation's largest junkyards could be set aside as national archives— monuments to what the nation has discarded. Autos and other machines could be classified by some sort of Dewey decimal system and curators hired to give guided tours or conduct the operation as a drive-in museum.

Today's junkyards are becoming overcrowded since seven million vehicular skins are shed yearly. One proposal that has attracted interest is to charge Automan 2 percent of the purchase price of the car as a sort of prepayment of funeral and burial expenses. Junked autos are reusable, but salvaging the steel for today's steel furnaces is too expensive to be profitable. Needed to complete the reproductive cycle are gigantic car eaters such as the one on Terminal Island near Los Angeles which can cannibalize fourteen hundred cars daily and produce scrap metal pure enough to be used in recycling.

THE FUTURE OF THE AUTO

Q. *Is the time coming when the country will have all the cars it wants or can use?*

A. (James Roche, former chairman of General Motors as reported in the *U.S. News & World Report*): We don't think so . . .

Q. *But isn't there a limit to the number of cars, in terms of roads and parking, in places such as N.Y.C.?*

A. Obviously, we have to find a way to take care of the growing number of cars. We're going to have to find parking facilities, build roads, throughways, freeways— whatever you want to call them—to accommodate this growth.

Roche describes the automobile as a growing organism or population. If the automobile is growing at the rate of about 4 percent yearly, then it is obvious we will have to build more roads and parking places. The mechanical-sexual population explosion of the auto is simply something to which civilization must adapt.

In the auto's future will be the proponents of population control and planned autohood instead of planned obsolescence. A sort of Malthusian rule of auto population exists since each new auto decreases available resources as well as the livability of the environment. Our children's children will study in their history books about that unique time that ended in the late seventies or early eighties called automania. It will be compared to previous intoxications with the railroads and ships, each acting as a Trojan horse bearing desirable gifts but introducing an unforeseen scale of change into the lives of the recipients of its graces.

Our recent history in legislation, city planning and taxes has so overemphasized the auto that the time has come to pay for the excesses of the past. Even a high priest of the auto religion, a Ford vice-president, has admitted that ". . . more and more people view the automobile as an unfortunate necessity." Since almost everyone has an auto, other consumer products—snowmobiles, bikes, boats, trailers—fulfill the need for status symbols, and nonpossession could become the most elite status symbol.

The limited supplies of center city space and energy makes the auto's future dim. Automobiles will not disappear. They will rather become mere transportation devices, not mechanical centaurs or marriage partners. Like the horse today, the future of the automobile might lie in recreation while more practical social solutions to transportation are found.

Patterns of auto ownership in the future might resemble that of today's supermarket shopping carts. Small cars, inexpensive, slow and all alike could be left in holding areas available for whoever needed one to use and leave at a different area. Long-distance transportation would be done by rail or other more efficient people carriers. The two-car garage attached to every house will give way as a status symbol to the no-cars-allowed planned developments.

Automan rides off into the sunset not far from the twilight of the auto-god and demise of the mechanical centaur but still with years of turbulent life ahead.

Last summer I drove from Chicago to California and back. From that trip I experienced the sameness of the country as seen on a road map. The auto hasn't made travel possible, it has destroyed the experience of travel. It has helped homogenize the land with McDonald's, Howard Johnson's, Holiday Inns, green and white signs, Top 40 radio and restaurants and gas stations giving free candy with every fill-up. Travel is indicated by the odometer and the fact that the view through the windshield keeps moving like some never-ending film.

My mind was filled with Exit, 55 mph, Stop, city and street names, No Littering, Food-Gas-Lodging, Keep Right, Wrong Way, Do Not Pass, Slow—and I realized that my world is not necessarily enlarged by the number of miles I have traveled.

Forced to ride through unchanging Nebraska as an obstacle to California, I recalled a Sandburg poem and lived a variation of it. I was riding on a limited-access expressway, Interstate 80, one of the best in the nation. Hurling across the prairie into blue haze and dark air, I was part of two unending lines of steel containers holding thousands of people (all the cars will one day be scrap and rust and all the men and women laughing and talking will pass to ashes). I stopped and asked a man in a diner where he was going and he answered, "Omaha."

Chapter 4

Advertising:
The Engineers of Illusion

Back in Bicentennial 1976 we all had at least one good laugh at the red, white and blue wastebaskets, the toilet seats with George Washington's picture and even the patriotic coffin called the "Spirit of '76" offered by one Indiana casket manufacturer. We read magazine articles or saw fillers on the TV news about buy-centennial promotions and counted the Bicentennial minutes until 1977 mercifully rescued us from such exuberant excesses. In looking back, we realize how much we enjoyed feeling superior to those "gullible" consumers who spent millions on anything imaginable that was somehow presented as patriotic. We, of course, are much too civilized to have rushed out and installed a new twenty-foot flag pole on the front lawn or to have purchased for the kid's room a rug with pictures from American history of two hundred years ago. But any manufacturer worth his or her stars and stripes made money by applying judicious dabs of red, white and blue paint. Who did buy the 148 tons (a figure derived by less than scientific means) of so-called patriotic merchandise produced in 1975-76? The promiscuous purchaser, of course.

The promiscuous purchaser is one of two types of people classified according to their response to advertising. The second type is the group of the "personally immune," a group to which, no doubt, you, the reader and I, the writer, belong. But let's deal with these two types in order of interest—promiscuity before immunity.

Members of the first group, the promiscuous purchasers, rush out to buy 50 percent of all the products they see advertised. These highly ad-responsive individuals have helped to make advertising a highly successful multibillion-dollar-a-year industry. The only problem with promiscuous purchasers, other than their constantly overdrawn checking accounts, is that they are a very elusive group to locate and study—even more so than that group of voters who twice elected Richard Nixon President of the United States. This group is also known by the unofficial name of "suckers," and one well-publicized study conducted many years ago revealed that the group is growing at the approximate rate of one new member every minute. However, the method of measuring this group's growth has been questioned, and it could be true that the "promiscuous purchaser" exists primarily in the minds of the people in the second group. Let us take a look at these members of the second group, basking in the warm glow of immunity.

The second group, the personally immune, consider most ads (especially those on TV) dumb, silly, "beneath my dignity," and generally a waste of time. Members of this group can sometimes be heard to say, "Ads seldom influence my opinion; I am an informed consumer who knows true value when I see it." Ads, this group believes, are evidently aimed at those unfortunate members, people of group number one, who rush out and purchase promiscuously. Strangely enough, 90 percent of the nation's adults believe themselves members of the "personally immune." This same 90 percent accounts for approximately 90 percent of all purchases of advertised products—obviously something is amiss.

The problem is that the belief in personal immunity from the influence of advertising is the first group's great weakness. A person who believes himself or herself immune will not take defensive action, will not protect against exposure. The result of this weakness is a hidden susceptibility to advertising that leads to pseudo-choice in the marketplace as well as unwitting exposure to the values of education-by-advertising.

To illustrate the myth of personal immunity, we need only look at the "prune problem." Prunes, alas, have a bad image; people make jokes about prunes, call enemies "prune face" and generally consider the wrinkled fruit more a competition for Ex-Lax than for peaches or Twinkies. Perhaps because of their poor image, prune sales were declining about 1 percent monthly when the Prune Advisory Board decided to hire an advertising agency to lift the lowly prune to new heights of acceptability.

The agency ran the following radio ad in eighteen American cities:

(door chimes)

WOMAN: Yes? Who is it?

MAN: Hi. I'm your new neighbor, Steven Williams in 107.

WOMAN: Oh, how nice to meet you . . . well come on in . . . it's a pleasure.

MAN: Thank you.

WOMAN: I see you've got a measuring cup. Now let me guess . . . you ran out of sugar.

MAN: No.

WOMAN: You're a bachelor . . .

MAN: No *(laughter)*, as a matter of fact—I was wondering if I could borrow some prunes.

WOMAN: Prunes? *(laughter)* I'm sorry . . .

MAN: Well, yeah . . . I thought a couple . . .

ANNOUNCER: There are still a lot of people who laugh at prunes. But now quite a few are finding out how good they really are. Because pound for pound, prunes have eight times the Vitamin A of the leading fresh fruit . . . and more iron, niacin, and Vitamin B2 than the five leading fresh fruits. They're also a great natural source of quick energy.

WOMAN: He wants to borrow a cup of prunes? *(uncontrollable laughter)*.

MAN: Thanks anyway . . . maybe I'll try 105.

WOMAN: Yeah . . . *(laughter)*
ANNOUNCER: California prunes, the funny fruit that does so much for you.

If you were to position yourself at the prune display in a supermarket in any of the eighteen cities targeted for advertising and ask people why they are buying prunes, you would hear some strange answers. You would certainly have a difficult day and perhaps even collect a few strange looks and maybe a bruise or two, but you would *not* hear people reply, "Because of that persuasive ad I heard on the radio." Yet, sales increased an amazing 18 percent in the cities where the ad was used. Prune sales in cities where the ad was not used continued their typical 1 percent decline.

The California Milk Producers Association shared with prune growers the problem of a decline in consumption. For fourteen consecutive years per capita milk consumption in California had declined. Two years after an ad agency was hired to conduct a "milk is good for you" campaign, Californians were drinking 5 percent more milk.

Both ad campaigns were successful in changing behavior patterns of large groups of people and both campaigns worked so subtly that users were not aware they were under the influence of advertising. Although the decision to eat more prunes or drink more milk is among the best that advertising could prompt, the fact is that people were influenced behaviorally without awareness of the source of the influence. The myth of personal immunity has led to a condition in which much, if not most, advertising operates on a subliminal level. Behavior patterns are changed without full awareness, and choices thus made fall into the realm of pseudo-choice.

Eating a few more prunes or drinking milk after leaving the crib will harm no one, not even in the pocketbook. But sometimes, advertising leads to a pseudo-choice that is irrational, expensive and very likely useless to the purchaser. One such example is the ongoing ad war waged for the money spent masking smelly mouths. Mouthwash advertising is a major factor (if not *the* factor) leading to the expenditure of over $300 million yearly for a substance that has been thoroughly proven to be of little more value than plain water.

The mouthwash advertising war heated up back in 1963, a time when mouthwash and Listerine were almost synonymous. Americans spent only $115 million on mouthwash in that year, and Johnson and Johnson introduced Micrin to steal some of the millions from Listerine. Fourteen years and over $50 million later, Warner-Lambert's Listerine still rules the oral battleground, holding down over a 50 percent share of the market. Johnson & Johnson's Micrin holds down only a few percentage points of the total market while Procter & Gamble's Scope enjoys 20 percent (these figures might be changed considerably by the time you read this).

All the shots that have been fired in the advertising war have caused some mouthwashes to sell better than others, but that has not been the most profound influence in American life-styles. The major influence of tens of millions of advertising dollars has been to triple the total amount of mouthwash used. All the advertising has convinced Americans that mouthwash is useful and desirable.

Almost every technique in the adman's bag—from exploitation of the need to be accepted to scare tactics—have been used. Even the package on the shelf is an ad. Bright colors, clear liquids and shiny bottles seem to be part of the attraction of mouthwashes on the drugstore shelves. The "natural" color of mouthwash is more like water (this is not surprising since alcohol and water constitute the main ingredients), but bottles of water-like liquid are hardly a strong selling point. So the color psychologists are called in. As *Advertising Age* comments: "Lavoris positions itself with a vivid red, the hottest hue in the spectrum and the one with the highest action-motivation quotient. Red also has a strong masculine appeal. The blue favored by the old Micrin is the most widely appealing color; it is cool, sometimes even cold, color that generally soothes, relaxes, inducing leisure and contemplation. The yellow of Listerine is warm, yet there is definitely an antiseptic feel to the shade used. Obviously, by intent."

All the pretty colors and millions of dollars result in a few corporate giants splitting a $300 million take each year. Currently, most of that money goes to Warner-Lambert (Listerine), Johnson & Johnson (Micrin), Procter & Gamble (Scope), Vick Chemical Company (Lavoris) and Colgate-Palmolive (Colgate 100). What do these companies provide in return?

The consumer pays about $9 per gallon for a solution whose main active ingredient is alcohol (5 to 25 percent). In 1971, the Federal Trade Commission challenged all medicinal claims for mouthwashes and complained that the claim of Listerine to "kill germs by the millions on contact" is of no medical significance. The ad-educated consumer is willing to pay four times more for mouthwash than for milk in spite of a study conducted by the National Academy of Sciences which found that "There is no convincing evidence that any medicated mouthwash, used as part of a daily hygiene regimen, has therapeutic advantage over a physiologic saline solution (salt water) or even water."

If consumers would rely on a book such as the *Handbook of Non-Prescription Drugs* instead of advertising for knowledge of bad breath cures, they would find, "While no one doubts that bad breath can be offensive, there is some doubt as to whether a mouthwash is the solution to the problem. . . . many manufacturers include antibacterial agents in their products. Claims that an antibacterial can kill during the short duration of the average gargle must be viewed with a jaundiced eye. Secondly, the lining of the mouth is protein and the quaternary ammonium compounds used in many mouthwashes are absorbed and partially deactivated by protein."

Or for further evidence as to the value of those colored bottles of alcohol water, the Council on Dental Therapeutics of the American Dental Association found that, "Even claims that mouthwashes overcome mouth odors should be viewed with some reserve . . . No method is yet available to give a thoroughly satisfactory comparison of germicidal agents in a test tube with the same agents under the actual conditions of their use in the oral cavity. There is no adequate evidence that the average normal person benefits by a nonspecific change in the oral flora. Considerable uncertainty exists concerning the role of microorganisms as etiologic agents of oral disease."

So mouthwashes *might* be more effective than water but no more so than salt water. But advertising has taught that mouthwash can work wonders. Even in drugstores where a house brand is available with the same ingredients as a heavily advertised brand, the name brand will easily outsell the house brand. This is true even if the name brand is double the price of the store brand.

The psychological danger of mouthwash use is minimal, but it is undoubtedly part of the obsession with personal-care products and hygiene that advertising both encourages and exploits. Medically, the use of mouthwash is harmless, although it could be used to cover symptoms of more serious problems that should receive immediate medical attention. Economically, the net effect of mouthwash advertising is to direct $300 million a year into the hands of a few corporations in return for a liquid of, at best, questionable value.

Advertising has left millions of Americans "freely" choosing to spend millions among various brands of a product about which they know nothing; their decision has been reduced to the level of pseudo-choice.

The illusion of personal immunity leads to pseudo-choice not only among the various necessities and niceties of daily life, but also in regard to the medium of advertising itself. We are so convinced of our immunity to advertising that we allow it to become omniscient and invisible. We accept ads as part of the environment, like wind and clouds, and have given up the choice to be free from ads.

In 1975, TWA experimented with commercials during its programmed in-flight music available to passengers with a headset. Advertisers paid $5000 per month for one sixty-second ad on each of the seven in-flight channels every hour. During the successful test period about one million listeners heard the ads and TWA reported only twenty-eight complaints. We have come to accept ads as creatures that inhabit any possible space capable of supporting a printed or spoken message.

In his book, *The Paradise Program*, Anthony Haden-Guest tells of the problems Coca-Cola has experienced because of its status as part of the environment. Coca-Cola management found that people could walk down a street with as many as forty or fifty Coke signs yet not remember having seen even one. A Japanese dissident hijacked an airplane and demanded to be flown to North Vietnam. Officials decided to remove all signs of capitalism from the South Vietnam airport and land the hijacker there where he could walk into the welcoming arms of the police. When the plane was about to land, the hijacker threatened to shoot the pilot unless he took to the air again. The airport subterfuge almost worked but a Coca-

Cola sign was left uncovered—it had become so much a part of the environment to the people at the airport that it became "invisible."

Advertising abhors an empty space. Highway billboards, banners and signs at athletic stadiums, plugs in feature films, movie shorts before the feature that are little more than extended ads, signs on buses, trucks, windows (when was the last time you were able to see inside a supermarket window?), newspapers and magazines containing 85 percent advertising, city streets choked by a cacophony of conflicting print styles and colors, and oranges with a brand name imprinted on each peel have become an accepted part of ordinary life. We cannot easily choose to be free from advertising for a day or a week, to enjoy the absence of someone calling our attention to a new improved cigarette or old aged whiskey.

Precisely because we are so literate our eyes are drawn to print, to words in any environment. To demonstrate to yourself how word addiction works, try going through an ordinary day without reading or listening to ads. As you drive to work, read only the signs necessary for your safety. Chances are the effort needed to undo your entrenched habits will be too much to sustain for any period of time. And so we are denied chances to discover the value of silence and nothingness, an environment conducive to contemplation. Advertising has taken quiet away from us, has made the choice impossible. Our minds become jammed with bits and pieces of jingles, buzz words, products, ad images, brand names and slogans so there is no room for meditation and little room for self-confrontation. The omnipresence and repetition of ads drive out thoughts that question the need for the products advertised and fill the space that might otherwise be used to construct a solid value system that might reject much of what is advertised.

The positive value of silence is replaced by an environment of misinformation. Advertising also contributes to pseudo-choice by supplying misinformation that leads to ill-informed purchasing decisions that can be described only as pseudo-choice. For example, advertising contributes to eater's alienation by failing to provide useful nutritional information about food and by overemphasizing the synthetic "junk food." The prune and milk ads mentioned earlier are refreshing exceptions to this trend. Automotive advertising distracts drivers from considerations of safe, economical cars by insisting on appeals to status and feelings of power.

Advertising has become the nation's leading source of health and hygiene education. About one of eight TV commercials is for drugs and four of TV's top ten advertisers are drug manufacturers. Constant repetition of long-running campaigns have taught older Americans to spend millions in search of the perfect and utterly regular bowel movement. An FDA study found that one-third of Americans believe the myth that it is medically necessary to have a daily bowel movement. Ads have encouraged the spending of millions yearly on mouthwashes of little or no value. A study by the American Dental Association found only two brands of toothpaste to have any value beyond that inherent in brushing; yet Americans have learned that their smiles will be sexier and their dentist bills lower by using any one of the dozens of other pastes on the market. Iron deficiency anemia was second only to the common cold until Geritol was finally required to end its campaign of misinformation.

Americans spend nearly a half billion dollars yearly for relief or cure of the common cold. Much of the expense for antihistamines and various combination remedies is prompted by advertising. What advertising does *not* teach about the cold is that (a) there is no cure for the common cold, (b) our best chances are to keep in good physical condition, eat well, take sufficient fluids, keep clean and rest and (c) various over-the-counter drugs for the cold relieve symptoms but hinder the body's natural defense against the cold, thereby inviting a longer cold or complications leading to pneumonia. Antihistamines, for example, do indeed reduce swelling to provide a modicum of breathing relief. But they also interfere with white corpuscles that serve to defend the body against invading viruses that caused the cold in the first place.

Back in 1966, the Food and Drug Administration invited a panel of experts to examine the safety and effectiveness of over-the-counter drugs. The National Academy of Sciences' National Research Council was the group charged with reviewing the efficacy of consumer drug remedies.

The panel of that committee charged with the study of cold and cough remedies was headed by Dr. Philip S. Norman, a specialist in allergies and infectious diseases associated with the common cold. According to Paul and Rene Murphey, writing in *The Village Voice* of April 12, 1976, "Dr. Norman told us that the panel concluded in its report to the FDA that Contac and Allerest were *both* ineffective and unsafe, and that Dristan was ineffective; furthermore, that Contac and Allerest should not be sold either over-the-counter or by prescription." He based the recommendation for the ban on the possible side effects of the preparations which include glaucoma, urinary retention, obstruction of the respiratory tract and even symptoms of schizophrenia.

The Senate Subcommittee on Monopoly offers support to Dr. Norman when it concluded, "Medical and pharmaceutical experts state that no convincing evidence of benefit has yet been presented for the oral use of these drugs to relieve nasal congestion in colds." The American Medical Association has issued a statement that "In most instances these combination products (Contac, Allerest, Dristan, Coricidin) have more sales appeal than actual usefulness. Often they are irrational or even dangerous." Advertising can educate, persuade and offer pseudo-choices that are irrational. The nation's bill for over-the-counter cough and cold remedies is nearly $1 billion dollars annually.

The FDA has not publicly released the 1966 report, claiming that "only 420" products were studied out of a field of thousands. In the best traditions of obstructionist bureaucracy, it has since established another panel to take the recommendation of the earlier panel under consideration.

Cough and cold remedies are not an exception to the rest of the over-the-counter drug selection. Hundreds of antacid preparations are available in drugstores, and their advertising has been among the most humorous and creative on television from marshmallowed meatballs to talking pink stomachs and acid-shredded napkins that supposedly represent the stomach lining. The antacid ads do not remind sufferers that any persistent pain in the lower chest or stomach should be checked by a physician even if it does respond to an Alka-Seltzer and seem to be "only gasid indigestion." The ads do not encourage sufferers to ask what their stomachs are trying to communicate about eating habits.

In spite of well-publicized studies showing that aspirin is aspirin, the buying public insists on paying up to four times as much for brand-name aspirin from large drug companies. Consumers pay more than $100 million a year for the privilege of brand-name aspirin and aspirin combination.

The aspirin market is controlled by a few large drug companies that advertise heavily and charge at least double what nonadvertised brands do for aspirin. Sterling Drug's Bayer aspirin once claimed in advertising "all aspirin is not alike." Bayer claimed in its own tests that "for quality, Bayer proved superior." What the tests showed is not that Bayer works better against headaches but that it is whiter and less breakable than some other tablets. Whitehall Drug Company's Anacin claimed that it "provides a higher level of pain reliever" and accompanied the claim with a chart superimposed over a human head. Anacin did not make clear that the extra pain "reliever" does not provide extra pain "relief." The extra pain reliever was simply a bigger pill. If the "illusion" was given that it was a better aspirin, it must be the fault of the audience's misunderstanding.

Ads that told the truth about aspirin and combination pain relievers were prepared by a law firm for free use by interested magazines—few established publications accepted the ads even though they offered a valuable public service.

The danger in analgesics advertising is not that a consumer might buy one product instead of another. The danger is that the consumer learns about pain relief from commercials and is, therefore, almost totally ignorant of facts and at the mercy of pseudo-choice in the drugstore. Millions of Americans have spent long hours in the school of advertising and have learned that pills can work magic, changing toads into princesses in a mere thirty seconds.

Many over-the-counter pain remedies are rated by the FDA as "probably ineffective" or at best no better than plain aspirin. Yet millions of satisfied customers swear by the properties of various brands of combination drugs so often advertised on television. A study by physicians found Compoz no more effective than a sugar pill. The FDA has found that Cope is no more effective than aspirin and that it will not relieve nervous tension or anxiety. Yet millions find that these drugs do indeed fulfill their advertising claims.

What the scientific analysis does not take into consideration is that many drug users are also educated advertising listeners; they believe ads. The effect of many drugs is closely linked to the patient's belief in their power; the placebo effect is well established in medical history. Even though the products advertised are chemically ineffective, they work because of the belief caused by advertising. By this Alice-in-Wonderlandish logic, brand-name drugs are more effective than nonadvertised brands.

Consumers learn not only about health and hygiene, odorology and hair care from advertising, they also learn a far more basic lesson of pseudo-choice—buy brand names. This lesson costs dearly. Heavily advertised products can sell for 50–200 percent more than the same ingredients in a less well-known brand.

In 1964, Tenneco hired an ad agency to sell bananas. The agency decided that bananas lacked "brand identification" and coined "Chiquita Banana" as the key to a $16-million ad campaign. One year later a survey revealed that 49 percent of shoppers actually preferred Chiquita bananas and would pay a premium for them.

In a year-long study at a Chicago food chain twice as many people bought a certain brand of margarine under a well-known brand name as the identical margarine sold under the store brand, even though the store brand was less expensive.

Large oil companies spend millions in developing brand-name loyalty for customers' gasoline dollar. Gasoline, another parity product, is basically all alike, yet drivers will pay 5 cents a gallon more for the brand name than for the same gas sold down the block at a station with a name never seen on television or in magazine ads. Ads train consumers to pay for more advertising.

The overall effect of advertising as a source of education is to give and withhold knowledge so selectively as to create the illusion of a knowledgeable choice but the reality of pseudo-choice. In fact, advertising as it exists today could accurately be described as a craft that uses language and images to create the illusion of superiority. Certainly there are truly superior products that ads honestly describe, but this is not how the bulk of advertising money is directed.

Advertising is not so much the engine of the economy as it is in adman's Howard Gossage's words, "A $17 billion sledgehammer to drive a 49¢ thumbtack." Half the national expenditures for advertising goes for items that account for only 5 percent of the GNP and about 2 percent of the labor market. Most advertising is done for consumer products that are indistinguishable from each other; the money is needed to create the illusion of uniqueness and superiority. Products such as cereals, soaps, cosmetics, hair oils, toothpastes, deodorants, cigarettes and liquors pull in the biggest ad dollars. The more the products are the same (at parity with each other), the more the Madison Avenue magicians are needed to weave their word and image magic.

In ads the words and images are integrated into a total message. But for the sake of study and diffusing their power, we can consider the two elements separately. For advertisers have taken to heart the words of Humpty Dumpty, "When I use a word, it means just what I choose it to mean—neither more nor less."

The illusion of superiority among parity products is maintained by the careful use of language in the best traditions of wonderland. In parity ads the word "better" often means "superior to" while the word "best" means only "equal to." According to legal tradition any parity product can claim to be best. "Standard gasoline—the best you can buy," and "Minute Maid orange juice is the best made" are both valid claims since neither one claims any kind of superiority to competing brands. "Best" means "as good as." To understand the ad definition of "best," one must translate it as "no better or worse than the competition." The word better, however, is dangerous to use. Standard could not say, "Standard gasoline is better than any other gasoline." Nor could Minute Maid claim to be "better than any other orange juice." The legal interpretation is that such claims are for superiority and cannot be made unless the product is truly superior. The word "better" is often used without a referent. Minute Maid could say "the better breakfast drink" or Standard could say "better for your car," since neither says what they claim to be better than.

One of the most useful tools of the creators of advertising illusions is the weasel word. A weasel word is one that weakens a statement or deprives it of real meaning. It is an equivocal word designed to avoid a firm commitment to the truth. A "weasel word" is named after the habits of the weasel. The weasel is an animal capable of sucking the contents out of a raw egg without doing apparent damage to the shell. When the farmer comes to collect the eggs, he discovers the weaseled egg only when it is handled. An egg attacked by a weasel looks like the real thing but upon closer inspection is empty and hollow. An advertising claim containing a weasel word looks like a statement of some real advantage but upon closer examination is a hollow statement without meaning.

Some of the most commonly used weasels are:

helps
fights (*also acts or works*)
controls
as much as
up to
from (*as in "priced from $14.95"*)
the feel of or the look of
best and better
many or most
subjective words (*words giving opinions of taste or appearance—
    delicious, smooth, luxurious, etc.*)

Sometimes weasels are used to deceive and mislead the casual listener or reader. But other times weasels are used because few things in the world are absolute. A claim such as "cleans *most* hard-to-clean dishes" is a recognition of the fact that a baking pan might be so devastated that nothing short of steel wool or dynamite could clean it. No cleaning agent cleans "everything."

Weasel words have been used as a selling technique long before mass media and advertising. What is unique about weasel words today is that, like advertising itself, they are so overused as to become invisible. Even the "personally immune" listener tunes out the weasel words. An oil company will introduce a new kind of motor oil and claim it will provide "up to ten more miles per tankful of gas." The vast majority of people who hear the ad understand it as claiming the oil will give them ten more miles per tankful. The weasel "up to" is tuned out. The oil might give ten more miles per tankful to a very limited number of specialized engines and do very little or nothing for the average car. The "up to" weasel serves both to keep the claim honest and to mislead the casual ad reader or listener. A closer look at how weasel words suck the meaning from advertising claims appears below.

Weasel Claim	Claim with Weasel "Tuned Out"	Explanation
"*Acts* against hay fever misery"	"Cures hay fever"	If any product could "cure" hay fever it would advertise that ability with absolute clarity.
"*Helps control* dandruff symptoms"	"Stops dandruff"	Washing with plain water also "helps control" dandruff. The question is how much control? A hat "controls" dandruff.
"A luxurious *wood-grain look*"	"Made of wood"	"*Wood-grain look*" translates as paper, plastic or metal treated to look somewhat like wood. A "*Wood-grain look*" is no more "wood" than a photograph of a tree.
"*From* $14.95"	"Priced from $15 to $33"	Even the well-established practice of using 95 cents as part of a price is a bit of a weasel. The hope is that mentally a price like $14.95 sounds more like $14 than a straight $15. Gasoline prices of 60.9 cents a gallon are really 61 cents but that .9 makes customers think in terms of a 60 cents gallon. The "from" is printed in tiny letters. The phrase "and up" is used for the same purpose.
"Chocolate-*flavored* ice cream"	"Chocolate ice cream"	Ice cream with no chocolate in it at all cannot be called chocolate ice cream. But if artificial flavoring and coloring are used it can still be "chocolate-

		flavored ice cream" even if it contains no chocolate.
"*Helps* make *soft* nails hard and chip *resistant*"	"Hardens nails so they won't chip"	How much does it help? Does it help "normal" nails or only "soft" nails? How soft do nails have to be to be hardened? Any nails "resist" chipping but they are not chip proof. Also be careful not to confuse "water resistant" with "waterproof."
"Gives you a higher level of pain reliever"	"More pain relief"	Is more pain reliever more effective? Does more pain reliever provide more pain relief?
". . . the *delicious taste* of peaches" or "Real peach flavor"	"Real peaches"	Delicious, fresh, luxurious and similar adjectives are mere opinions. There are no standards for these words. Anyone can claim a food is fresh or delicious. "Taste of peaches" could mean peach flavoring rather than real peaches.

Weasels are not the only advertising technique used to engineer pseudo-choice and increase the level of misinformation in the environment. The demonstration ad is one of the oldest techniques known to advertisers. A Tonka toy ad demonstrates the durability of its toy by showing an elephant standing on a toy dump truck; American Tourister luggage allows a gorilla to throw around a suitcase that escapes undamaged; and Saab hires a stunt driver to roll a car down a hill and drive it away unscathed, or Xerox demonstrates the quickness of its typewriter by racing it against an IBM and winning easily. Demonstration ads can be among the most convincing, but they can also be among the most misleading.

A fine example of how a demonstration can scrupulously avoid telling an outright lie yet manage to give what some might consider a deceptive impression is provided by an ad for Procter & Gamble's Bounty paper towels.

Bounty towels account for about 20 percent of the paper towel market primarily because P & G spends from $6 to $7 million a year to advertise the quicker-picker-upper. In a recent series of TV ads Rosie the waitress, played by Nancy Walker, demonstrates the "two cups and saucers trick." Rosie wets a piece of Bounty and asks her customer to put two coffee cups and two saucers onto the towel. Miraculously, the soggy Bounty supports the weight.

The trick to the demonstration lies not in the strength of the towel but in how it is held. If the towel is held by its perforations (with the grain), it will support weight—as will many other paper towels. If the towel is held against the grain, it will not support the weight—luckily Rosie holds the towel the proper way. The demonstration does not actually lie but neither does it tell the whole truth. Viewers who conclude that Bounty is the strongest towel this side of a beach blanket are basing their decision on a deceptive demonstration. Almost any two-ply paper towel may work as well for Rosie in her demonstration.

In an ad for STP, the motor oil additive and thickening agent, a class in consumer education was used as a foil for a demonstration that proved nothing but implied wonders. The ad told of a letter that a high-school consumer-education class wrote to STP. In the letter the class described an experiment in which a screwdriver was dipped in oil and students attempted to lift the oil-slickened tool by grasping the metal end with two fingers. With oil, they were able to lift the screwdriver, but when the tool was dipped in STP, it defied the efforts of the class to lift it without slipping.

Supposedly, the ad demonstrated that STP makes oil more slippery or lessens friction to a greater extent than oil. The class concluded that STP works as the manufacturer claims. But the class fell victim to an error in logic and a hidden assumption. All they tested was the ability of STP to make screwdrivers slippery. Since the product is sold to put into automobiles, and not to make tools slippery, the class tested the product in a manner utterly irrelevant to its actual use. There is no sound reason to conclude from the screwdriver experiment anything except that STP is slipperier than oil when applied to screwdrivers. The class (and, by extension, the viewers of the ad) ignored the real use of the product and its possible negative effects on engines.

An ad for Saran Wrap demonstrates that it is tougher than the competition (shown by a box labeled "ordinary wrap") by means of a bit of subterfuge. A woman tests "ordinary wrap" by running her finger through, easily piercing the transparent wrap. When another woman tries the "same" test with Saran Wrap, she is unable to break the "Saran barrier." A close examination of the TV spot shows that with the "ordinary wrap" the woman uses a fingernail long enough to have her arrested for possession of a lethal weapon. For Saran Wrap only a rounded and soft fingertip is unable to poke through. The only fact the commercial demonstrates is that a fingernail is sharper than a fingertip.

These three demonstrations do not prove that the products are inferior. Bounty and Saran Wrap may indeed be stronger than some of their competitors and STP might help some engines. But the "scientific" demonstrations of the products exist in the world of shadowy half-truths and give consumers only misinformation. Purchasing decisions based on such half-truths are more likely to be pseudo-choices than those based on totally honest and helpful demonstrations or facts.

In 1972, the Federal Trade Commission hired an independent testing organization to evaluate ad claims by seven automakers and found that the data behind two out of three claims were not adequate. Of fifty-four technical claims, twenty were classified as "grossly inadequate or actually contradicted the claim," and fifteen others were "relevant but inadequate." Chrysler's claims for greater comfort from torsion-bar suspension was called "historical recitations devoid of comparative data." General Motors' claims of extra safety from side door beams were characterized as unsubstantiated. Ford's LTD comparison of noise levels with a Mercedes were found to be similar enough so that the average listener would find the difference unnoticeable.

In 1971, the FTC asked companies to substantiate claims of 282 ads. Only 40 percent of the claims were satisfactorily documented by advertisers. Ford claimed its LTD was "over 700% quieter." The substantiation for this claim showed that the comparison of LTD's quietness with "some of the world's most expensive cars" included comparing new 1966 LTDs with nine used European touring cars. The "700% quieter" turned out to mean that the inside of the car was 700 percent quieter than the outside. If readers thought the claim meant that the car was 700 percent quieter than other cars, they misunderstood the ad's intent.

Chevrolet Chevelle's claim of "109 advantages to keep it from becoming old before its time" included antipollution and safety items (like backup lights) required by law and other items that were standard equipment—rearview mirrors, balanced wheels and tires, an automatic choke and even a "full line of models."

Weasels and demonstrations fail even to suggest the vast range of techniques that advertisers can use to ensure the consumer's confinement to pseudo-choice. For example, auto manufacturers often advertise "special limited editions" of cars with special features or paint stripes at supposedly reduced prices. But such an offer might not be a sale at all, it might be a way of selling a "stripped-down" car. Ford Motor Company recently offered a "limited edition" Mercury Monarch at "$250 off regular sticker prices." The cars were described as being a "limited edition," and "specially equipped with new bench seat and interior trim . . . available in three feature colors." To most people a limited edition, a term borrowed from the world of publishing or art, indicates something of greater value and desirability. But the Monarch "limited edition" consisted of a regular Monarch with a cheaper bench seat substituted for bucket seats, less costly interior trim, a limitation of three choices in exterior colors, and a less expensive steering wheel. Ford took $250 worth of parts from the car and charged $250 less—hardly a sale in the traditional sense and certainly not a highly desirable "classic design" or "artistic masterpiece" that the term "limited edition" implies.

After analyzing these few ad claims that appeal primarily to the mind, let us take a closer look at the techniques used to appeal to emotions and psychology—psychosell.

Social critics often blame cultural mirrors for their accurate but unflattering reflection just as the Greeks blamed messengers for bringing bad news. Advertising is a reflective medium that often reveals more about the audience than the product. Advertising reflects the findings of motivational research, painstaking surveys and studies and the results of carefully designed experiments testing consumer behavior. Some of what advertising reflects are those parts of ourselves and our national character that we normally hide from ourselves; *we* are the hidden persuaders, not the ad creators. An anthropologist from the future wishing to study the American character could do far worse than begin by reading or viewing a few thousand typical commercials.

The harshest critics of advertising who dub it corporate brainwashing might be entirely accurate in their critiques, but they fail to see the value of advertising as a social indicator. Daniel Boorstin in *The Image* compares this viewpoint to the eighteenth-century English and American attitude toward insanity. Unable to understand the mentally diseased, "normal" people saw in them something wicked to be locked up and beaten. It wasn't until the twentieth century that the various forms of insanity were recognized as merely extreme examples of tendencies in each of us "normal" people. Only with this latter insight were we able to understand both insanity and normality better. Boorstin points out:

> *Similarly with advertising. Baffled and suspicious, we deride the witch doctors of Madison Avenue. It is they, we say, who want to involve us in the figments of their disordered imaginations. They lie to us; they persuade us against our will. Accusing them, we fail to see what their activities can teach us about ourselves.*

Putting aside blinding criticisms and feelings about advertising, we can see ads as reflections of our national psychology. Ads often exploit holes in the national personality. We can either condemn the exploitation or use the ads to see the holes more clearly—or both.

Humans are symbol-makers and abstractionists who give meanings to things. Advertisers are not responsible for this phenomenon; it exists in cultures where advertising does not. Primitive tribes have status symbols; a row of pots on the roof of a hut can symbolize a successful provider just as clearly as a Cadillac in the driveway. But advertisers do attach psychological labels to objects and present them as capable of filling certain personality holes.

Coca-Cola promises the "real thing" not only to counter a Seven-Up "Uncola" campaign but also because phoniness and artificiality are so much a part of our culture. Pepsi "helps 'em come alive" only because there are so many people out of touch with themselves and feeling a deadness inside. Countless products from beer to boots promise masculinity (and define it as well) because there are so many males who have serious doubts about their sexual identity.

After viewing a thousand ads and commercials (equivalent to the number seen by an average person in three days), two basic personality holes might be quite evident—the lack of genuinely pleasurable experiences and the absence of self-acceptance. It is these holes that advertisers have found most lucrative and most exploitable.

Ads that illustrate and imply fun, excitement, adventure and pleasure are among the most common precisely because these experiences are missing from so many lives. Just as the well person does not constantly ask himself how he feels, the society with a healthy amount of pleasurable experience would not respond to such advertising. A truly pleasure-loving society would be invulnerable to the illusory promises presented in ads for soft drinks, alcoholic beverages, franchise food or hundreds of other products. There would be no room for a communications system to tell citizens that a cigarette will help them come "alive with pleasure" or a beer will enable them to "reach for all the gusto you can" or that a soft drink can "add life."

A national virtue of self-acceptance would send the ad world into turmoil. For ads that promise to provide a measure of indirect self-acceptance are legion. A most common kind of ad shows the owner or user of a product being accepted by others. This need for approval, acceptance and even status is a sign of the lack of self-acceptance. A self-accepting individual will still use soap, wear clothes and drive an automobile but his or her use of these items is not prompted by the need to gain acceptance—there is no hole to fill. Advertising that associates approval by neighbors and friends, members of the opposite sex and society in general with products thrives only where self-acceptance is lacking.

Ads not only reflect the national psychology, they also educate. H. G. Wells's fictional advertising man, Dickon Clissold, had the right idea:

"Advertising; what is it? Education. Modern Education, nothing more or less. The airs schoolmasters and college dons give themselves are extraordinary. They think they're the only people who teach. We teach ten times as much . . .

"The only use I've got for schools now is to fit people to read advertisements. After that, we take over. Yes, we—the advertisers."

From the seller's viewpoint advertising is persuasion; from the buyer's viewpoint it is education. No single group of people spends as much time or money per lesson to educate the masses as do the creators of ads.

Ads participate in a feedback loop. They reflect a society they have helped to educate, and part of the advertising reflection is the effect of the advertising itself. Every ad that exploits a personality hole educates the audience toward using a particular product to fill that hole. Just as drug ads teach a crude and sometimes dangerous form of self-medication, psychosell ads teach a form of self-analysis and cure for psychological problems.

An ad that stirs a hidden doubt, that causes a person to ask, "Why does no one love me?"; "Why don't I have more friends?"; "Why am I lonely?" invariably goes on to suggest a partial cure—use our product. If an announcer for Pepsi would appear on screen and say:

"Are you lonely? Do you feel left out? Do you sometimes feel that everybody else has all the fun in life? Are you bored and isolated? Well, if you are, drink Pepsi and find yourself instantly a part of all those energetic, joyful, young-at-heart people who also drink Pepsi."

Such an ad would be greeted as either laughable or insulting by the viewing audience. Yet the old "Pepsi generation" campaign used pictures and a jingle to make exactly such a point.

The danger in psychosell techniques is not that people might switch from Coke to Pepsi in soft-drink loyalties or abandon Scope for Listerine. The danger is that millions learn (especially if the message is repeated often enough, as ads are) that problems in self-acceptance and boredom can be alleviated by corporate products. Which brand to buy is secondary to ads as education; the primary lesson is that the product itself satisfies psychological needs.

This is a dangerous doctrine, for as long as masses of people believe that personality holes can be filled by items bought in stores it matters little which brands they buy. The failure of the gospel of advertising to solve problems merely leads people on to buy a reportedly more effective or prestigious brand (be it a car, house or perfume) rather than to question their motives for the original purchase. Psychosell ads educate us to look "out there" for solutions instead of within. Advertising promotes and thrives on the neurosis that passes for normality. Ads teach that personal failures can be avoided by things almost as a witch doctor promises magic charms to cure illnesses. By so doing they contribute to mass neurosis and alienation as well as pseudo-choice. Our most effective means of education sell instant solutions instead of the motivation needed to gain psychological maturity. The danger of the "hidden persuaders" is not that they are seldom noticed, but that they help to keep ourself hidden.

If one pages through some old magazines rescued from the basement, a few psychosell techniques stand out. An ad for jeeps shows a lone man in a red jeep from a very low camera angle. The jeep seems almost to be flying against the backdrop of a blue sky with a few massive clouds. The ground looks more like a wheat field with a crew cut, and the picture is obviously an artist's drawing rather than a photograph. The headline pasted over the sky is "The Great Escape." The ad is typical, neither especially creative nor unusually perceptive.

The promise of a "great escape" would hardly be worth the thousands of dollars the magazine page costs unless there are a great many people who feel a need to escape. The ad appeals to those who feel imprisoned. Its headline probes that part of each of us that feels trapped—perhaps by work or family responsibilities or the problems of being human. The ad visually promises that a jeep will provide freedom.

The picture evokes the dream of wide-open space and the freedom of the frontier and a man alone on his trusted horse. The name of the jeep model, the copy tells us, is "Renegade," carrying further both the wild West theme and the escape from boredom—who ever heard of a bored renegade? The buyer of a jeep can share the dream of the early Americans to escape to the uncivilized lands of the wild West. The combination of a man and his machine facing the wide-open spaces is often used in ads for snowmobiles, autos, motorcycles, recreational vehicles and boats. In many of the ads the machine is presented as a surrogate horse or woman (or both) and the promise of freedom and excitement is at least implied.

The copy in the jeep ad reads:

> *Comin' at you—the famous Jeep CJ-5, the ultimate get-up-an'-go machine. Get a hold of one of these babies, like this sporty Jeep Renegade and you're in for the ride of your life.*
>
> *She was born to run free far from the pavement. Built to take hard knocks in her stride, the Renegade boasts a brawny suspension, heavy duty axles and a tight 32.9 ft. turning diameter. Roll bar, fender tip extensions and special aluminum wheels come with this spirited beauty.*
>
> *. . . '74 Jeep Renegade for a really great escape.*

It would be quite easy to dismiss the copy as embarrassing writing by a frustrated poet. But it would be more accurate to consider ad copy a form of poetry—call it pecuniary poetry. Aldous Huxley recognized that, "The advertisement is one of the most interesting and difficult of modern literary forms." Semanticist S. I. Hayakawa agrees that advertising is a form of poetry. Both use strict economy of language, paying careful attention to the slightest connotations and emotional effects of the words chosen. Both use intentional ambiguity to add meaning on multiple levels. Both advertising and poetry strive to give the objects of daily experience meanings beyond themselves. Ad writers, like poets, must invest things with significance since man is a maker and buyer of symbols more than things. The task of the copywriter is to poeticize consumer goods.

The jeep copy is intentionally ambiguous. Much of the copy can be applied not only to the product, but also to a woman. The jeep is "baby," "*she* was born" and is a "spirited beauty" who will give you the "ride of your life" if you are so lucky as to be able to "get a hold of one of these babies." And since the woman thus categorized would hardly be a feminist, the reader notes she is "built to take hard knocks in her stride." Of course, much of the copy could also be applied with some accuracy to a horse.

Considering the ad as education, we find it teaches that escape is equivalent to freedom. The jeep does not provide freedom, only its illusion. Freedom is not the possession of a machine that enables one to ride in fields on weekends. The ad teaches that freedom is the ability to afford occasional escape from whatever is preventing freedom. Ads, such as the psychosexual one for jeep, according to Erich Fromm in *Escape from Freedom*, "give . . . satisfaction by their daydreaming qualities just as the movies do, but at the same time they increase his feeling of smallness and powerlessness."

A few pages later in the magazine (which, by the way, contains more pages of advertising than editorial content) the same theme is repeated in a Yamaha ad with the headline "The great getaway machines." This ad shows romantic couples rather than a man alone but promises that the cycles will help the rider "leave behind the regimented week that was." The ad continues the theme of using a machine to rediscover the delights of Eden.

Lane furniture has a small ad showing a couple in a New York high rise, standing at the bedroom door admiring each other or the Lane bedroom set. The headline asks, "Furniture or modern art?" and the copy answers, "It's both." The ad cautions potential buyers not to "be surprised if your friends view it as a work of art." The bedroom set is quite attractive but the illusion spun is that it has something to do with art. The furniture is mass produced and the woodlike carved surface is molded plastic. The pattern is given the out-West name of "Pueblo." The ad is a bit of art education (and where else can a casual reader obtain art education?) both denigrating the concept of art and strengthening the hold of kitsch.

The illusions that ads create are dangerous insofar as they are an education system that teaches us to look out there, into the marketplace, to solve problems and enhance our self-image. They are also dangerous because, as Alfred Korzybski, the founder of general semantics, points out, "Human beings are a symbolic class of life. Those who rule our symbols, rule us."

Chapter 5
The Packaged Environment: Illusions of Quality and Culture

Packaging is one of the most influential factors in the engineering of everyday pseudo-choice. Packaging should not be confused with its more basic predecessor—packing. A product is "packed" in order to transport or store it safely for any length of time. The development of the United States through a rapid westward migration and its original settlement across an entire ocean made the pioneers experts in packing. Packing was as essential a skill to the settlement of the United States as packaging is to the activity and expansion of today's economy.

In early America, barrels, boxes and bags were used in grocery stores to contain and preserve, not to sell. It was not until the early 1900s that the word "to package" entered the American mindset as a verb rather than a noun. In 1899, Uneeda biscuits set a precedent that was to shape the future of choice in America. Uneeda deserted the traditional cracker barrel in favor of a folding paperboard box that served all the purposes of the cracker barrel and also worked as an advertisement. As recently as the 1920s, most supermarket purchases were packed rather than packaged. But today packaging has become an essential part of the formula for any product's success; sometimes the part of packaging is more crucial than the quality of the product itself.

Between 1958 and 1971, the production of packaging in the United States increased 71 percent. Over one-half of all paper production, 87 percent of all glass production, 20 percent of plastics, 14 percent of aluminum and 9 percent of all steel production goes for containers. In fact, packaging consumes 5 percent of all the energy used in the entire nation. In spite of this vast growth in packaging, things to put into packages have not kept pace. The result is that we are faced with an ever-increasing display of psychopackaging to the extent that many packages cost more than the products they contain. In the food industry, for example, between 1963 and 1971, consumption of food per capita increased a mere 2.3 percent, but food packaging increased 33 percent by weight per capita. Instead of offering consumers a choice of better quality in products, producers are increasingly tempted to offer ever more seductive packaging instead.

We have already seen in the chapter on food that the sense of taste has atrophied enough so that a change in packages will actually cause a purchaser to change his or her perception of the contents. A beer packaged (and advertised) to appeal as a premium brand will taste better to a majority of drinkers than a beer with drab or neutral packaging. Bread wrappers determine if the purchaser perceives the contents as fresh or somewhat stale.

What we call "impulse buying" is little more than buying packaging. As Daniel Boorstin points out in *The Americans: The Democratic Experience*, ". . . people went to the supermarket hoping to be seduced into buying something they 'really wanted'. In England and elsewhere in the Old World, it was still true in the late Twentieth Century that middle class shoppers went to market to *buy* what they wanted, while Americans went increasingly to *see* what they wanted. " And what they saw was an explosion of packaging that often replaced quality and true choice with illusion.

The corner grocery store died what many view an early death not because of smallness or inefficiency, but because food producers realized the power of packaging to sell itself if constructed with the proper psychological hooks. The small corner store was doomed when Clarence Saunders of Memphis, Tennessee, opened a grocery store in 1916 that made the entire store a packaging device. Saunders gave his store the unlikely name of Piggly Wiggly. His innovation was to admit customers through a turnstile and then channel them around the store through a maze of well-stocked aisles past the merchandise and finally out past the check-out counter. Previously, shoppers came to stores with lists and picked out some items themselves and allowed the grocer or his helper to select the rest. Often a long pole with a mechanical hand was needed even to reach the floor-to-ceiling shelves. Since much of the merchandise was out of the customer's reach, purchases based on impulse were few.

But at Piggly Wiggly, the shopper served himself or herself and the grocer serviced the shelves. This system forced shoppers past enticing displays of food they had not considered for purchase before entering the store. The maze-of-aisles-self-service system led to impulse buying and the demise of carefully planned menus. The Piggly Wiggly revolution was such a success that various studies show that about 70 percent of all supermarket purchases are now based on impulse.

The importance of the sudden impulse to buy leads to a new science of decision engineering, of channeling the impulses of shoppers so they conform to the situation of highest profits for the corporate store owner and food manufacturer. It is no longer surprising for more time and money to be spent on the development of a new package than on research for improved products.

Gerald Stahl, director of his own package-design firm, explains what is needed in the grocery store: "The average woman takes exactly 20 seconds to cover one aisle in a supermarket; so you have to have a carton that attracts and hypnotizes this woman, like waving a flashlight in front of her eyes. What will hypnotize her? The colors red and yellow, at the moment. But if the majority of cartons are covered with these hues, then the trick is to use another color. We've done one product in white—looks like nothing all by itself, but surrounded by red and yellow boxes it really stands out."

Red is the best signaling color, green is second and yellow third. Yellow can make a container appear larger than other colors when used in large areas. A red-yellow combination is an aggressive, attention-getting device. Blue is the color people most often report as "my favorite." A yellow-red-blue combination should therefore be attractive for much packaging and, in fact, is used quite often. These three colors are the most used in packaging.

A surprisingly recent discovery among food packagers is that a highly appealing photograph of the food can be used on the package with greater impact than the name of the brand in any combination of colors. A "serving suggestion" of the end product—for example, a can of mushrooms showing the sautéed mushrooms smothering a steak—inspires the imagination of a potential purchaser much more effectively than abstract words. The dreamlike pictures have a primacy over verbal symbols.

A close look at a number of food packages reveals some of the other techniques of visual and semantic confusion in packaging that contributes to pseudo-choice. Our earlier tour of the supermarket revealed products such as Polynesian-style frozen dinner, gourmet instant coffee, watered-down chili and skim milk soufflé with spinach that illustrate the placing of psycho-packaging techniques before the needs of customers. But less esoteric foods are also subject to the persuasion of packaging.

A package of twelve frozen blueberry waffles carries the name of its corporate maker, Quaker Oats, only in tiny print on the side of the package. Featured on the front in picture and large print name is a smiling and thoroughly modern Aunt Jemima. Quaker Oats research has no doubt shown that the image of the Southern "mammy" goes well with the waffle product. The largest picture on the package shows three of the waffles smothered in syrup and butter. In the background is a basket of blueberries; all the items appear larger than life. Perhaps the real reason the blueberries are shown only in the background is that the waffles do not contain whole blueberries. In a red oval insert on the package front are the large words "made with real blueberry buds." Presumably the casual shopper is supposed to combine the words "real blueberry" and the picture of the blueberries on the front to expect the waffles to contain real, whole blueberries.

A blueberry bud is certainly not what you might think it would be—the flower of a blueberry tree. It seems to be some kind of process by which the flow of a blueberry syrup can be controlled during the manufacturing process so that it can be injected into the waffles as spots of blue. For some reason, Quaker wants no part of whole blueberries. The main ingredient in the waffles is water. How many Aunt Jemimas would make waffles with water as the main ingredient?

Packaging is the tool used to support the work of the food alchemists. Packaging enables the alchemists to create foods that imitate other foods but are made with inexpensive ingredients. Aunt Jemima waffles are a fine example. They sell for about 90 cents per pound yet have water as the main ingredient. Nowhere in recipe books can one find a recipe for waffles that uses water as the main ingredient. Some other products that have water as the main ingredient but are accepted because of their advertising and packaging are:

Lemon cream pie (frozen—80 cents for a one-pound pie that melts if left out of the freezer too long. It contains no cream and only lemon juice instead of lemons.

Baby food—fruit dessert, chocolate custard pudding, oatmeal with applesauce and bananas are only a few of the baby foods with water as the major ingredient.

Crème de menthe syrup—a gourmet's delight for special desserts. The eight ounces of liquid sells for $1.07, yet contains sugar water with artificial flavoring.

Fruit drinks—fruit "drinks" should not be confused with "fruit juice." The Minnesota Department of Agriculture tested orange drinks for juice content and found that "brand names" such as Del Monte contained only 9 percent juice, Libby's a paltry 6 percent and Coca-Cola's Hi-C only 9 percent juice.

Frozen nondairy creamer
Pepper Oriental
Chocolate eclair
Creme puffs
Cheese ravioli
Frozen turkey dinner
Frozen Mexican dinner

NOTE: not all brands of the above foods contain water as their main ingredient.

The right name for a product is important. No one would buy a potato dinner but he or she might buy a man-sized portion of potatoes. According to consumer activist David Sanford, General Mills tested a new food called Mexican Macaroni. The product failed, not because people wanted a spicier taste, but because the name was wrong. General Mills changed the name from Mexican Macaroni to Macaroni Montabello and all was well.

The larger-than-life pictures, carefully chosen descriptions and names, and the psychologically correct colors all combine in the science of psychopackaging.

Food and other personal items have to give the illusion of being protected from anything "unclean." Motivation researcher Ernest Dichter points out, "Packaging makes things 'holy.' Many people do not want to be reminded of the 'animal' nature of food items." This fact leads to much overpackaging in the form of protective wrappings.

The final shape of a package is sometimes psychologically determined. Studies have found that soup products are better received when they are packaged in a round form. Round cartons are generally preferred in ice cream also. In box-shaped cartons a kind of "psychological roundness" can be created by design; for example, by printing a ribbon around the square container. A strong design on the bottom of the container was also found to help allay the consumer's fear of melted ice cream leaking.

Ernest Dichter comments in his book *Packaging: The Sixth Sense?* that ". . . in a study on lipsticks, we found the more phallic the lipstick and the packaging appeared, the more it attracted women—but one has to be careful not to go overboard and make parallels too obvious."

He also says that men "fall" for exaggerated, idealized designs on a package more than do women. Men will buy plastic containers of nails and screws in a hardware store even though they may never have any use for all they purchase. Dichter explains that "the psychological explanation is a feeling of wanting to be a provider, to have a stockpile of things at home for the occasion that may arise."

The grocery store itself is a kind of environmental package designed to encourage a shopper to buy the high-profit, impulse items. A common device used in many supermarkets is to greet the entering shopper with a display of low-cost "specials" carefully positioned near the entrance or the place where grocery carts are stored. These specials are not necessarily "best buys"; the key element is that they be low cost—preferably items of 30 cents or less. Such a display overcomes the shopper's resistance to high food prices and creates the habit of reaching for unplanned items. Hopefully this habit will carry over into more profitable displays.

Also near the entrance will be some kind of good smell if at all possible—baked goods are often used to give a pleasant aroma to the store and whet the shopper's appetite. Muzak plays softly in the background to soothe the shopper's nerves and help lull him or her into a mood of acquiescence to the lure of the packages and displays. Most shoppers enter for basic food items—meat, produce, dairy items and bread. These basic foods are often placed around the outside walls of the store to move the shopper around the building and ensure that the end-of-aisle displays are seen. If a store were to be arranged for the convenience of the shopper, the most often bought items would all be located close to the entrance for those who wish to purchase only a few of the basics. But this would narrow the scope of possible impulse purchases and decrease store income.

Customers have to be led through as many linear feet of shelf space as possible so the packages can do their selling. As shoppers maneuver baskets, they are confronted by a variety of special p-o-p promotions displays to encourage more buying. Food manufacturers and producers sometimes sponsor contests with elaborate prizes going to the best displays. The Florida Department of Citrus sponsored a contest in which every grocer who sent a photograph of his citrus display would receive a bonus check from $2 to $500, plus a chance to win cars, TV sets, video equipment and other big prizes.

The special displays and in-store signs do help move groceries. Even a simple sign saying "as advertised" on a shelf near a specific food will increase sales of that item by an average of 65 percent over advertising alone without the sign. Comparisons between stores selling the same product show that the store that features it as part of a well-designed p-o-p (point of purchase) will sell two to four times as many as the store where it is simply displayed on the shelf.

Shelves must be kept as fully stocked as possible; researchers have found that empty shelves can cut sales by as much as 20 percent. Shoppers confronted with nearly empty shelves have the feeling of being able to choose only from remnants or the rejects of previous shoppers.

Campbell's carefully instructs grocers to stack their soups more vertically than horizontally. According to Campbell's, sales increase 5 to 26 percent when the soup cans are stacked up rather than across.

High-profit, impulse items should be placed at eye level. Lower shelf space is the least desirable and should be left for items people "need." Little racks (called "extenders" and attached to shelves) contain a few special items and increase sales. A study by *Progressive Grocer* found that ". . . a well-planned extender program could easily add over $15,000 in extra yearly sales for supermarkets in the $35,000 to $40,000 volume range."

Candy for adults is an impulse item and so is often placed in racks near the checkout counter to work its effects when customers wait in line. Lower shelves are good for appeal to children. *Progressive Grocer* reminds storekeepers that "In candy, sales increases in ranges of 14% to 39% have resulted in the placement of multipacks of penny candies, of suckers and TV-advertised products on the bottom shelf within reach of the juvenile crowd." One store used the bottom shelf to great advantage for a liquid soap that had a whistle attached as a free premium. The soap was placed on the lower shelf within easy reach of kids and sales increased 22 percent.

The various ploys of packaging used in the supermarket work below the conscious level to influence the purchases of shoppers. The choice of foods is shaped by packaging and merchandising in an environment where overchoice is the surface appearance but pseudo-choice the reality.

The concept of "packaging" is certainly not limited to use in supermarkets. The basic idea of the package or the mode of presentation of a product as a sales device was popularized by the grocery industry and has since become one of the most influential choice-shapers in contemporary life. Packaging contributes to pseudo-choice by obscuring rather than revealing the true options. The package as sales device also helps place the initial purchase decision one step removed from the actual product.

From the supermarket, the idea of the importance of the package spread to other industries and areas of life. Today, packaging is not limited to a physical box or container for a product; it has become part of the merchandising process even for products that need no containers. Vacations are packaged, builders offer subdivision packages, furniture offers both design and package considerations, shopping has been packaged via shopping centers and even culture itself is packaged.

KITSCH: PACKAGED CULTURE

Money, as the cliché goes, cannot buy happiness. But the cliché would not exist if it did not express some degree of commonly accepted truth. Purchasable products can be "packaged" as happiness, love or culture. The psychological package is attractive to those looking for an easy way to obtain something they desire but either don't know how or are unwilling to exert the necessary effort and suffering to achieve it.

Kitsch can be defined as a package of phony culture. Kitsch is something ordinary, cheap or simply mass produced but packaged to appear as culture or art with a capital A. Webster's 3rd International Unabridged Dictionary defines kitsch as "artistic or literary material held to be of low quality, often produced to appeal to popular taste and marked especially by sentimentalism, sensationalism and slickness."

Kitsch is not merely failed art. Neither the flawed statue nor the mistakes of a beginning artist constitute kitsch. Nor is kitsch whatever the collective opinion of critics brands as "not good." In fact, let us avoid the adjectives "good" and "bad" since they are frequently used to hide more than they reveal and are rarely agreed upon by more than 1.4 persons at any one time.

The word "kitsch" is probably derived from the German "verkitschen"—to make cheap. Ludwig Giesz wrote a scholarly work titled *Phenomenologie des Kitsches* in which he arrived at the most unscholarly conclusion that kitsch is "artistic rubbish." We will not enter the bloody battlefield where art critics fight over the difference between trash and art. Here kitsch will not mean poor art, it will mean phony art—masquerade, packaged pseudo-culture.

Something is kitsch if it is made to appear cultured or artistic or profound or something it is not when in reality it is intended to appeal to mass tastes and the mass market. An ordinary mass-produced object (a bedspread, poster, towel, chair, etc.) becomes kitsch when some element is added in order to lend it an aura of good taste, urbanity and cultured sophistication. Kitsch provides instant pseudo-culture. Or, as we shall see later, instant pseudo-hipness or naturalness or historical authenticity. Kitsch appeals to those who lack personal standards of taste yet want to present a front of cultured tastefulness. The use of kitsch becomes a pseudo-choice only when the user believes the object of kitsch does in fact represent art or culture rather than merchandising.

Kitsch is what mass man consumes to indicate individuality, but in reality succeeds only in proclaiming that he is a creature of mass society. Kitsch is the child of the marriage between mass production and culture; it is inescapable in mass society.

Kitsch defies tidy definitions but invites examples. Before we embark on our guided tour, it will be necessary to explain that there are various kinds of kitsch. The types of kitsch are determined by cultural needs. We saw earlier in our consideration of psychosell techniques in advertising that a product can be advertised in such a way as to appear to fill one of a variety of "personality holes." Merchandisers turn objects into kitsch when they present them as packages that fill a cultural hole. The most common cultural needs or desires merchandised are the desire to appear cultured and/or artistic, patriotism, the need for a sense of historical roots and tradition, the desire to be considered "in" or "with it" and the desire to appear successful.

Each of these needs is difficult to meet in contemporary society and requires effort, time and knowledge to satisfy. But various products can be packaged in such a way as to give the illusion of satisfying these needs and desires. A person who wishes to present an image of cultured urbanity but who doesn't know a paint-by-numbers from a Picasso is likely to take the easy road to culture. A thick slipcase of records containing all the "world's greatest music," and a never-read coffee-table book of paintings by French Impressionists (bought from publishers' overstock for $8.95) help further the illusion of culture. The need for historical roots and stability might be helped by a living room filled with furniture that is sold as "traditional," "Colonial" or "Early American." The furniture is no more Early American than a French fry is a summary of French cuisine, but the illusion is what counts.

Kitsch is often a substitute for quality and is closely linked with the gradual disappearance of excellence in many areas. If the package can sell, there is less need for concern about the contents. The forces that make kitsch so much an inescapable part of the environment also lead to shoddy construction in automobiles and houses, mindless television entertainment and movies, bland textbooks and the tasteless food which has become a national trademark and epidemic.

In a mass culture, few products succeed unless accepted and paid for by huge numbers of people. A television show cannot afford to have an audience of only a few hundred thousand. A textbook cannot afford to risk rejection by state adoption commissions in ten states. A can of chili has to be bland and tasteless enough to offend no one. A general, if overstated, law of mass culture is that if everyone doesn't want it no one gets it. So everything from prime-time television to frozen food is aimed at the lowest level of acceptability. Exceptions are often geared to a moneyed elite. Because manufacturers and producers know that people want quality and fine things, kitsch enters the scene to help create the illusion of quality. Kitsch has replaced honest workmanship in many areas of choice.

Let us take another tour, this time in search of packaged culture. We leave our supermarket loaded with packages of we know not what, change into Automan and pick a freeway to the nearest suburb. Kitsch and packaged culture are not special privileges of the suburbs, but once there we can find a house with a statue on the front lawn and begin our tour.

As we come around Sunset Drive, we see the kind of statue we

take to mark the beginning of our kitsch tour. The plaster-cast
statue vaguely resembles a well-known classic masterpiece. It is
placed near the center of the front lawn and has a spotlight for night
illumination. The statue is not for enjoyment by those who live in
the house; from the front window only the back of the creation is
visible. It is there, we suspect, to impress passersby and visitors
with the fact that the residents can afford statuary and have cultured taste. The statue was purchased down the highway at The
Patio, an outdoor furniture store that specializes in marble
birdbaths. The statue is certainly not art, although there are
houses that have folk-art displays on the front lawn. Folk art comes
from the people; kitsch, like the statue, is imposed by mass producers in order to satisfy (or exploit) the cultural needs of the
masses. Less expensive versions of the statue include a black stable
boy in red and white, holding a lantern or the cut-rate kitsch
special, a pink plastic flamingo.

The owners of the house do not seem to be home, so thanks to
the craft of surreptitious entry let's enter the house in search of
more examples of packaged culture. Perhaps the owners are out to
dinner at some nearby restaurant. If they are, they probably feel at
home, since the environment is very likely a masquerade of
Polynesian, Olde English or Parisian, with food that is a frozen
dinner in disguise, culinary kitsch.

Upon entering the house, we look up and see a series of wooden
beams across the ceiling. Upon closer look we realize they are
Styrofoam, not wood. Using new technology as a design element
in furnishing is not kitsch in itself. What is kitsch about the
"beams" is their masquerade. One major merchandiser calls them
"antique timbers with a hand-hewn look." Such a description
degrades the word "antique." And that is one of the problems of
kitsch; it fails to treat what it imitates with respect. Thanks to mass
merchandising, "antique" has the vague meaning of something
that looks old or that wasn't purchased last week at the shopping
center.

Walking around the house we notice that the tendency of kitsch
to drive out the authentic is well illustrated in the collection of
lamps. The type of illumination provided by lamps and their
ability to create moods and influence the environment have been
almost totally neglected in favor of kitsch considerations. Homes

with nearly invisible built-in lighting seem limited to the very rich. Most lamps have some sort of *objet d'art* as a base, from which protrudes a pole with a light bulb and shade perched on top. The lamp bases in this house include a milk can, gum ball machine, vase (under $30 the base is pronounced vāse, over $30 and it becomes vāse), an imitation oil lamp and some sort of wire sculpture. In all fairness to the owners, it seems nearly impossible to obtain a simple source of room light that does not pretend to be a work of art or a reminder of our patriotic past or a throwback to the good old days.

Taking a peek into the bedroom we see a bedroom set with what looks like hand-carved surfaces. Very attractive, but on closer examination we see the element of handcarving is simply molded plastic glued onto what is possibly a particle-board surface. We recall seeing an ad for this particular bedroom set (in our study of psychosell advertising) that cautioned one not to "be surprised if your friends view it as a work of art."

In the "family room" (a description fast becoming a euphemism to describe the room with the largest TV set) is a six-foot-long "stereo hi-fi console" that looks like it was designed by a retired funeral parlor decorator. The "design" of the unit is "Mediterranean," no doubt based on pictures of the original stereo used by Columbus aboard the *Santa Maria*. The box is cheaply constructed and contains only minimal electronics and is far from "high fidelity." The unit appeals to those who wish a large piece of furniture for $189 and who have no ear for music.

Next to the cabinet is a slipcase of records containing "The world's greatest music." We recall an ad for the set (for only $9.95) that claimed the set would give "all the music your family will ever need." The records appear in quite good condition, perhaps played only once. The ad reminds us of a comment by Dorfles in his book, *Kitsch: The World of Bad Taste*. Kitsch, he observes, ". . . is a problem of individuals who believe that art should only produce pleasant, sugary feelings; or even that art should form a kind of condiment, a kind of background music, a decoration, a status symbol even, as a way of shining in one's social circle; in no case should it be a serious matter, a tiring exercise, an involved and critical activity." Maybe the ad was right.

The furniture in the house seems modeled on an "escape" motif with a bit of Colonial here, French provincial there or what is called "traditional" in yet another room. A furniture salesman explained to a Senate subcommittee that the word "traditional" was used so often so the customer could imagine whatever tradition he or she pleased. For those with a limited furniture budget, the avoidance of kitsch in furnishing a house is difficult. If one wants sturdy, comfortable and attractive furniture at a reasonable price, one must be prepared to look long and hard. What is most common is poorly made, mass-produced imitations and abominations sold for a price based on the illusion it creates rather than the materials and workmanship it contains. Furniture is seldom honest.

There are no doubt dozens, or hundreds, of other examples of kitsch throughout the house, but we had better leave before we are caught and prosecuted either for breaking and entering or criticizing the tastes of others. As we drive through the neighboring suburbs, we consider the sale of houses as a form of packaging.

HOUSES

The furniture industry shares many of the selling philosophies of the housing industry. Neither industry is content to offer a well-made product, honestly presented and clearly explained.

Kitsch often seems to be inversely related to the quality of the building. Instead of improved methods of construction that would lower costs, instead of improved materials and quality workmanship, the house shopper is given a pseudo-choice. Those looking for a new house can choose from one of limited types that builders all over the country offer. After looking at moderately priced new housing, one would think there is a master architect who has drawn a dozen or so plans that are offered throughout the country with only a few local variations. Sameness is the rule of housing, with variety left to kitsch touches.

Since there is little choice in the type of house and little room for personal touches, an overchoice is offered in kitsch details, beginning with the name. The name of the builder's development is

Timberlane Estates (meaning there are at least three trees on the property), La Fontaine (having no relation at all to France), La Salceda (fake Spanish), Normandy Village, Runaway Bay (no water in sight), Colony Country or La Hacienda Estates. Each of the several models has an equally unlikely merchandising name—Briarwood, Statesman, Manor, Rancho etc. The more expensive the house, the more desirable the name.

The names again reveal a concentration on the theme of escape into the past or a foreign country. The names often give an air of cultured gentility to a collection of standardized houses built in what was last year a cornfield. The name of a housing development could be based on some intrinsic factors of the area. The farmer who owned the land, the names of original settlers or the predominant type of tree at least give some information about the land. But a public relations name like Normandy Village serves only to rob inhabitants of knowledge about where they live and give instead a kitschy fake-French status appeal. Kitsch thus contributes to the destruction of a sense of rootedness and genuine tradition. Names given to suburban housing and condominium groupings are depressingly similar all over the country. It is almost as if the same architect responsible for the nation's housing hired one advertising firm to draw up a list of three hundred acceptable names. Each time a builder decides on a new development, he picks four models and one name from the list.

The house itself will likely contain some element of kitsch. Houses are offered in what profess to be ancient and/or European styles such as Tudor, Colonial, Dutch Colonial, Georgian or Spanish. So-called contemporary styles will be a "ranch house" or "California style," conjuring images of the wide-open spaces or the old frontier. In the absence of real choice, labels often satisfy the need for illusion.

Most builders work on the McDonald's principle—like a hamburger, housing is standardized and customers need to be convinced that the standard house is what they want. Some builders take the Burger King approach and say "have it your way." "Your way" is advertised as "custom homes." But "custom" means only a choice in the color of siding, tile in the bathroom, carpeting and various minor options. Sometimes the more important option to add or leave out a wall or finish a "basement" or "family room" is also included. Just as at Burger King, the choices are defined by the seller and not the buyer. One cannot order a hamburger on rye bread at Burger King any more than one can choose outside of one of the builder's four basic models at Sunset Ridge Estates. In merchandising, the word "custom" so often designates the presence of pseudo-choice. Could not a sturdy, attractive house be built for $30,000 that would offer a customer meaningful options beyond choosing "decorator colors" of either Malibu White or Sunset Gold for the refrigerator and dishwasher?

In the realm of choice, we have moved from an era in which all products were "custom made." The village shoemaker made a pair of shoes for his neighbor or the farmer down the road, a house was built from the materials on the building site and structured to fit the environment. But mass production and the discovery of packaging led to today's situation in which everything is built for the anonymous masses. Very little is built for some*one*, it is built for *any*one.

In housing, this means personal dignity, the true needs of the buyer, respect for the local traditions and building sites are ignored in favor of a package of illusions and pseudo-choices. The packaged house represents the fulfillment of Emerson's observations that ". . . things are in the saddle and ride mankind."

To choose the least offensive package, even to express delight at its discovery, is not the same as expressing a willful "this is what I want." But a free choice cannot be made unless one is willing to look at what is there instead of the illusion presented by the packaging. A person who believes the illusions offered by kitsch is one unable to distinguish between subtle variations in reality. The difference between a finely crafted wood table and one covered by a thin wood veneer over plywood are not noticed. The absence of the ability to discriminate is exploited by the masters of kitsch. Cardboard bread, instant coffee, wood-grained plastic, Con-tact paper, Styrofoam wood beams and corporate controlled music are the prices we pay for the lack of contact with the environment and the ability to distinguish between the real and the masquerade.

Kitsch is not a problem because many people enjoy what those who are "cultured" find repugnant. Kitsch is a problem because it is a symptom of what effect mass culture has on the individual.

Kitsch thrives when a state of near senselessness in individuals passes for normality.

Between "I like" and "I don't like," between good and bad and between agree and disagree, there are an infinite variety of possible responses. The kitschman is like the baby who either laughs in delight or howls in rage when something shiny is dangled in front of his or her face. The only difference is that the adult kitschman uses purchasing power to shape the boundaries of what it is possible for everyone to buy.

The hidden message of kitsch is that quality is no longer necessary. A product, be it a shoe or painting, need not be possessed of high quality, it needs only to be highly marketable and profitable. The inability to distinguish masquerade from reality is directly related to the general deterioration of the environment.

Perhaps the only remedy to the domination of kitsch is for schools to teach materialism. Americans are often condemned for being "materialists." Yet materialists are people who love material, who can appreciate quality in things and who are sensitive to the physical environment. By this standard we are far from materialists; perhaps we are abstractionists, more concerned with money than wealth and obsessed with using things to serve more abstract goals such as status, belonging, power or security. A materialist nation would not live amid a superabundance of kitsch.

The problem with kitsch is not merely a vague sense of moral outrage at phoniness. The problem is that decisions about how the objects that surround us are designed are made by merchandisers. Objects are designed to provide illusions and pseudo-choices instead of meeting the real needs of people. Truman Moore, in his excellent book, *Nouveaumania*, recognizes the danger of a kitsch environment when he observes, "Gore Vidal once made the remark that we become what we seem to be. In other words, appearances are the frontrunners of what will be. If the appearance of the country makes it seem that we have no sense of authenticity, or history, and we are driven by a compulsion to imitate, can we ever feel like 'real' people in an atmosphere that is increasingly artificial?" On the level of choice and freedom the question is, can we ever develop our powers of choice and discrimination if we are offered choices only between imitation Early American and imitation French provincial?

PACKAGED SHOPPING

Shopping has become one of the nation's favorite pastimes. And, increasingly, shopping is what takes place at the more than fourteen thousand mostly suburban shopping centers that surround the largest cities. Huge new centers offer shoppers more choice of goods than any one building in the history of the planet. But the environment is as packaged as the supermarket to ensure each shopper the maximum chance to spend money.

What the supermarket accomplishes by its labyrinthian corridors of packages, the shopping center does by anchoring. A center is anchored by the major department stores, each located at opposite ends. This means that shoppers can enter the big stores (who often control the center) directly from their car but will have to pass by the smaller shops in the process of moving from one department store to the next. The interior court must be attractive and offer tempting views of other shops that could be visited. But the interior cannot be too comfortable a resting place, for this might encourage "loitering" by teens or the elderly, and people sitting on benches and chairs are not spending money.

The council that controls a shopping center is usually dominated by the major tenants, who, in connection with an insurance company or other money sources, produce the cash needed to construct the center. The council controls the environment in the center so that it is lively and filled but always profitable. The shopping center environment is to consumption what Disneyland is to touring: carefully controlled and pleasant with profitability as the deciding factor.

One of the early attractions of shopping centers was the ability to control the suburban environment. It was not until the early 1970s that the Federal Trade Commission issued restraint-of-trade complaints against a few regional shopping centers. Center developers needed long-term commitments from major retailers in order to secure the needed financing. In order to attract the major stores the developers offered leases that permitted the stores to protect themselves against too much competition. The so-called anchor tenants were granted veto power over other tenants' leases and had a voice in determining what was sold and for how much throughout the center.

Marriott Corporation, a large food supplier at shopping centers, regularly agreed not to provide waitress service at its Roy Rogers fast-food outlet in return for complete control of all the fast-food outlets in the center. Marriott outlets include Hot Shoppe Cafeterias, Farrell's Ice Cream parlors, Big Boy restaurants, Sirloin and Saddle, Donuts Galore, Fairfield Farm kitchens and The Joshua Tree. Parklane Hosiery Company signed a number of leases agreeing to sell only hosiery. Its expansion to include other products such as leotards has always involved a battle. The success of the FTC and state prosecutions have led to an end of blatant exclusivity contracts. But the fact remains that shopping centers are a way to control shopping, to make sure the consumer dollar ultimately winds up in the hands of the large corporations and less with local or independent businesspeople.

Regional shopping centers offer less choice than is apparent. Just as food manufacturers use a variety of brand names that hide oligopoly control, shopping center stores give an impression of a group of local businessmen banding together to give shoppers a pleasant environment. In reality, large shopping centers throughout the nation bear a similarity of tenants that gives shoppers a sense of *déjà vu* as they visit various Westgates, Northpoints and Woodlands in other cities. The developer of a large shopping center is usually a national organization. Since the developer is not a local business, it is not surprising that the majority of tenants are not local either, even though the name of the store suggests a small business or an individual owner.

Few of the average shoppers (who typically spend an average of five hours a week at shopping centers) would think of going to Interco or U.S. Shoe Corporation or Genesco or the Brown Group for clothes. But Genesco is the Nashville, Tennessee, company that operates Flagg Shoes, Jarman's Shoes, Johnston & Murphy Shoes and Whitehouse & Hardy Men's Wear. All four of these stores are represented at Woodfield, near Chicago, the nation's largest enclosed shopping mall. There are eight men's shoe stores listed at Woodfield. Of the eight, three are Genesco outlets, two are from Interco (Florsheim and Thayer McNeil) and one is of the Brown Group (Regal Shoes; also represented in the mall with a women's shoe store called Air Step). Three other shoe stores (Wild Pair Chandler's and Baker) are owned by Edison. The apparent overchoice of shoes diminishes considerably when looked at from the viewpoint of corporate owners.

Shopping centers account for more than half of all retail sales in the country. They are devices whereby large corporations can ensure that they collect a substantial share of the consumer's dollar. So although a shopper can choose from a vast overchoice of shoes, he or she will be unlikely to go to a shopping center and support a local merchant. The shoe purchase dollar will most likely go to one of two or three shoe conglomerates, no matter which store is selected. The corporation operates two stores in order to achieve market segmentation, not in the name of competition.

The shopping center as corporate package also has a tightly controlled physical environment. Louis Redstone, a shopping center designer, writes that the physical space ". . . should strive for an intimate character and subdued atmosphere. The purpose is to have the shopper's eye attracted to the store displays." Designers of shopping centers are not concerned primarily with "good" design; they strive to create an environment that will attract people and keep them there in a mood conducive to spending.

Each store within the packaged shopping center is carefully displayed to attract. Impulse buying must be encouraged in the stores as much as in the aisles of the supermarket. The owner of a children's clothing store in a mall in San Jose had her store "improved" by a management consultant supplied by the center's developer. One month later sales were up nearly 200 percent because, "We made it fun for the customer to wander around the shop, from display to display, from idea to idea, from 'oh' to 'ah.' " The shopping center is a large package containing a series of small packages that contain, in turn, the packaged merchandise.

MUZAK

Part of the packaged environment in supermarkets and shopping centers is background music, and the most sophisticated supplier is Muzak Corporation. Muzak is normally thought of as a pleasant public service provided for the benefit of customers. In reality, it is a part of the carefully packaged environment designed to increase employee production and customer spending. Muzak should be unnoticed but should influence, according to a Muzak brochure, "your heartbeat, metabolism and respiration, energy and alertness" as well as "make you feel relaxed or excited." But the intended "victim" of Muzak must not be aware of its influence.

Muzak uses what it calls "Stimulus Progression" to shape the moods and energy levels of those within range. Programs come in fifteen-minute segments with an equal amount of silence in between. According to the brochure, each segment gives "a psychological 'lift'—a subconscious sense of forward movement which combats monotony, boredom and fatigue. This is done by programming musical selections in ascending order—from least stimulating to most stimulating. The stimulus value of each selection is determined by factors such as tempo, rhythm, instrumentation and orchestra size."

The stimulus varies at different times of the day. Morning music will be lively and bright as it will when afternoon sluggishness strikes. Music for a Friday is different and perhaps more calming than for a Monday when there is a greater need for worker stimulation.

Studies show that Muzak is liked both by employees and customers—and how could eighty million people a day be wrong? According to Muzak's own studies, the musically conditioned environment works. Production at an Alabama knitting mill improved by 9 percent once Muzak was installed, typists at Lever Brothers made 38.8 percent fewer mistakes and Eastern Airlines reports that the music improved tact and friendly conversation among switchboard operators at their reservations desk. Some schools even report that Muzak helps with discipline as well as learning.

Muzak helps the employees work more (and is therefore less expensive than hiring more employees to do the same amount of work) and keeps customers content to stay and buy more.

Muzak, the carefully controlled environment of the shopping center or the supermarket, the psychological packaging of food and the bundled pseudo-culture called kitsch all contribute to the presence of pseudo-choice. They are all hidden factors in the environment that influences decision making. Insofar as they are hidden, they act as subtle shapers of the decision process. Ernest Dichter sums up the relation of pseudo-choice to packaging when he observes, "Whatever your attitude toward modern psychology or psychoanalysis, it has been proved beyond any doubt that many of our daily decisions are governed by motivations over which we have no control and of which we are often quite unaware." The illusion that we are free from unnoticed influence renders us even more susceptible to pseudo-choice.

Chapter 6
The Institution Trap

Once upon a time there was a town linked to the outside world by only one paved road. Every morning, around sunrise, a crew of men in a huge orange truck arrived and scattered nails on that one road leading into town. No one knew why they did this. It was their job and it had always been that way.

Unsuspecting motorists invariably could be seen along the side of the road repairing flat tires. The townspeople didn't like these drivers making tire tracks in the shoulders of the road and slowing traffic. They finally asked the city council to do something about the problem of the huge influx of motorists with flat tires.

The city council responded quickly to the demands of the people by passing legislation that called for the construction of a service station along the road so motorists with flats could receive help changing tires. This proposal was greeted with joy by the people and the station was quickly constructed. Within a few months the station was in operation advertising its specialty.

Drivers pulled into the station by the dozens each day, thankful that the service was so conveniently located. The manager of the station became an honored citizen of the town. Young people who wanted to "help people" would often put their idealism into practice by working at the station.

The manager was a forward-looking individual who introduced various reforms at the station, improving the method used to fix the flats and building a bigger station to handle the ever-increasing amount of traffic.

But the number of needy motorists increased faster than the station could expand. And so the people of the town willingly taxed themselves more to build another station a little farther down the road. Certainly the two stations could handle all the flats.

The two stations more or less managed to keep up with the demand. Dissidents in the town would occasionally demonstrate against the stations; they demanded that the service stations do a better job. A few other townspeople saw that the problem would be solved if only those people would stop having flats, but such radicals were easily dismissed.

Meanwhile at 5:00 A.M. every morning the huge orange truck lumbered over nearby dirt roads and made its way to the one paved road. There its crew scattered the nails on the road for another day. It had always been that way.

This little parable might seem absurd, but it accurately describes how many of our institutions function. In response to some problem, "society" creates an institution which, like the flat-fixing service station, attempts to help the victims. If the problem is defined as "people with flat tires," then the obvious answer is to build a service station to fix the flats. So the victims in our society, the deviants, the poor, the young, the old and the ill are sent to institutions to be fixed up. But, like service stations, they deal not with causes but only the effects. Institutions that operate on a service-station mentality never touch the real problem.

Eighty percent of all felonies in the United States are committed by people who have been through a correctional institution. The U.S. Office of Education reports that the average IQ of high-school dropouts in some large cities is higher than that of those who remain in school. A Ralph Nader task force found that homes for the aged often were legalized ways to exploit a nearly defenseless minority and that 75 percent of the tax-funded "homes" failed to meet minimum Federal requirements. As long as seven years ago, a New York City health commissioner estimated that over one thousand poor people a month die for lack of medical care in spite of a $250 million budget.

A large portion of the taxpayer's dollar goes to the support of "filling station institutions" that treat effects rather than causes. The decision to institutionalize the treatment of symptoms and more or less ignore causes is a social pseudo-choice. Those who are selected to be "helped" by the institution often have no choice to reject the service nor can they choose a competing institution that is more likely to meet their specific problem. Social critic Edgar Friedenberg calls these people "constrict clientele" and observes, "All politically powerless persons are subject to redefinition as members of a social group, require the administration of service they may not refuse, on terms they are powerless to alter. Youth of school age, persons defined as criminal or mentally ill . . . all share this experience."

In our parable of the flat tires, the motorists' pseudo-choice was limited to changing their own tire or allowing the service station to do it. The townspeople exercised pseudo-choice by voting to tax themselves to support a second tire repair station. The townspeople, like the nation at large, failed to understand the nature of institutions.

Institutions can be a trap as easily as they can be a source of solutions to social problems. Reading newspaper headlines and exposés, studying presidential commission reports and keeping up with the growing bibliography of social criticism, one eventually comes to a rather startling conclusion. Institutions often contribute to the very problem they are founded to solve. Mental hospitals drive patients crazy, schools encourage stupidity, prisons teach crime, police and Defense Departments provoke violence, welfare encourages poverty.

All these institutions share characteristics that force them to become a trap rather than a solution. *Institutions tend to become resistant to change, self-perpetuating, socially addictive and dehumanizing.*

CHANGE RESISTANT

It is the nature of an institution to resist change. In segment number six ("A Digression") of Saul Bass's excellent short film *Why Man Creates*, two snails are conversing. One says to the other something like, "Did you ever stop to think that radical changes in society eventually become institutions which in turn resist radical changes in society?" The other snail answers simply, "No," and the first abandons his theory. The sequence is one of the most insightful and yet overlooked parts of the film. Institutions operate in society similar to the way chromosomes operate in evolution. Chromosomes pass along to future generations successful gene mutations. Institutions pass along to future generations successful social mutations.

To oversimplify, take the example of the giraffe. Presumably there was a time when the only available food was foliage located on trees. Those giraffes with long necks were able to reach the food and pass along the genes that favored long necks while the short-necked giraffes gradually starved to death. The chromosomes passed along preserved the gene mutation that produced the long necks. Fine for the giraffe. But let's say the environment changes to resemble a world made up entirely of low tunnels. The long-neck giraffe is now at a serious disadvantage and is even in danger of becoming extinct unless another gene mutation can be successfully preserved.

Institutions are often like giraffes in a world of tunnels. They are proud of their once useful long neck but now lack the equipment to adapt to a changing environment. They will blame the tunnels, ask for more money to study the problem or build longer tunnels but will never admit the obvious—they are no longer a successful social mutation that should be preserved.

So institutions are created to preserve some change society believes is desirable as well as to prevent further rapid changes that would be disruptive. Institutionalized religion, for example, preserves what were once radical changes in man's way of relating to God, governments preserve past changes in the relation of an individual to the social body, prisons and mental hospitals preserve a once radical and advantageous solution to the problem of unacceptable behavior.

Since the institution is established to preserve a change, it resists further change by its very nature. The longer it survives and the faster society changes, the more obsolete becomes the change it preserves.

SELF-PERPETUATING

It is ironic but true that the most effective way to increase the local crime rate is to hire more police. More police will invariably account for a larger number of arrests and tickets whether or not the number of crimes committed increases. With more arrests being made, the statistics will indicate that the crime rate is increasing. With the crime rate increasing, the need for more police is obvious. But more police make more arrests and cause the crime rate to go up. So, in one sense, the law-enforcement institution causes the very problem it was created to solve. The same effect is present in most any institution that measures its needs and accomplishments by statistics. Train more psychiatrists and build more mental hospitals and the statistics will show an increase in the number of "mentally disturbed" Americans; build more prisons and there will be more prisoners; more hospitals will produce more patients as well as more doctors. The number of institutional "clients" expands to fill the available institutional capacity.

This tendency to grow is part of the institution's natural desire to preserve its own existence. One of the most basic, but invariably unstated, goals of any institution is to keep itself in existence. If the problem the institution was created to deal with can be shown to be increasing, the institution stands to receive more money, prestige, importance and power. This is not an evil conspiracy but a simple fact of institutional life. It would seem logical that if mental illness or crime increases, the institution would be judged a failure and be replaced. But this logic fails to take into consideration the fact that the institutions are socially addictive.

SOCIALLY ADDICTIVE

In addition to being self-perpetuating, institutions are socially addictive. This means that the first reaction to signs of institutional failure is to prescribe larger doses of institutional treatment. If one service station cannot cope with all the punctured tires, a second is built. A prisoner who is released and returns to crime is sent back to prison for more of the same treatment that failed to reform him or her once before. If, after twelve years of schooling, kids are not able to cope with "the complexities of technological society," we keep them there for four or eight more years. If a patient is released from an asylum and suffers a relapse, he or she is sent back to the asylum. The thought that the institution might actually contribute to the problem never seems to occur. Society becomes "addicted" to the institutions.

DEHUMANIZING

A fourth tendency of institutions is the most dangerous and the most avoidable. An institution often tends to dehumanize those within its care. This is especially true of "total institutions." A total institution has been defined by Erving Goffman in his *Asylums* as ". . . a place of residence and work where a large number of like-situated individuals, cut off from the wider society for an appreciable period of time, together lead an enclosed, formally administered round of life." Some examples of total institutions are concentration camps, prisons, boarding schools, monasteries or convents, certain military camps or an army at war, nursing homes, orphanages, ships at sea and many mental hospitals. The greater the institution's control of an individual, the more likely is it that some dehumanization will take place.

Schools are not, strictly speaking, total institutions but they do fit the description for the time the student is "in attendance" and they are a constant factor for so many years they often share this tendency to dehumanize.

Those who administer the institutions have no desire to dehumanize and very likely are unable to see the process taking place. Dehumanizing factors creep quietly and softly into institutions and are invariably introduced in the name of the "good of the individual." Not all total institutions dehumanize all of the time, but it is probably safe to say that all total institutions dehumanize some of the time. Enough research has been conducted to show that the failing is sufficiently widespread to warrant concern and study. To the extent that institutions allow dehumanization to take place, they contribute to the very problem they were founded to solve.

The research of Thomas Vail *(Dehumanization and the Institutional Career)*, Russell Barton *(Institutional Neurosis)* and Erving Goffman *(Asylums)* points to the following as among the most common institutional forces contributing to dehumanization.

- A new recruit (prisoner, patient, student, whatever) becomes just one of the group and begins to feel less like an individual and more like one of the batch. People are assigned labels, numbers, groups, wards, units, etc., and are referred to constantly by these labels. The individual is frequently reminded of his or her position as a group member.

- A small group governs a large group. Many dehumanizing factors are introduced simply because of this structure. Many institutional structures exist because of the need for a small group to govern (read: "help," "control," "improve," "teach" or "cure") a larger group. The two groups are segregated (usually with separate washrooms, eating facilities and rest lounges) and the governing group considers itself as superior.

- Rules and regulations supposedly introduced for the good of the individual often are in reality for the convenience of the staff. Rules for everyone are often made because of what one person did at one time. For example, a prisoner once stabbed a guard with a ball-point pen so prisoners are allowed only soft lead pencils. Rules tend to perpetuate themselves and exist unexamined.

- The atmosphere tends to be drab or sterile. Designs reflect easy maintenance and security rather than pleasant or humanizing living conditions. Fences, bars and walls are common. Fluorescent lighting, long hallways, bells, many clocks and a general feeling of hardness and coldness prevail.

- There are various restrictions on the freedom of movement and limitations on the choice of friends. Rules are instituted that make it easier for the institution to keep track of its members.

- Privacy is rare. There is no place to be alone.

- There exists some form of censorship, either of incoming publications, media, mail or publications produced by the members.
- There are large group gatherings at which attendance is required of all, even though all might not be involved.
- There is an elaborate system of rewards and punishments. The philosophy of the carrot and the stick rules.
- The staff tends to be bossy or domineering and hostile.
- Enforced idleness and boredom are common.
- Food is below standard and unappetizing. There is usually griping about food.
- Conformity with rules is identified with improvement and is often the only way "out" of the institution. Behavior is more important than cure or learning or the ability to fight or whatever the institution is supposed to do.
- Dress and hair are often problems. Hair is often cut upon entrance into the institution or regulated as to length. Dress is either regulated or made uniform.
- Drugs are used often. They are either freely chosen by the inmates as an escape or prescribed by those in charge as a control measure. Drugs are used not so much to make the individual feel *better* as they are to enable him or her to feel *less*.
- Routines, schedules and timetables are strict and extremely important. Time is divided into specially identified units such as periods, classes, shifts, watches, etc. Confinement or exposure to the institution is often measured in time units.
- There is a form of social caste either formally established or existing informally. Pecking orders are important.
- Information flow from the staff to the members is restricted. Staff usually knows much more than they admit to knowing.
- There is an entrance ritual. Life history, photo and ID card, weighing, fingerprinting, assigning numbers, searching, storing personal possessions, undressing, bathing, hair-cutting, assigning of rooms or places, and instruction as to rules and quarters.
- There is a restriction or total elimination of sexual activity.
- Staying out of trouble is likely to require persistent and conscious efforts. The avoidance of possible incidents determines certain decisions.

Note in all the above factors that each one can probably be justified within a specific institution, yet their cumulative effect is dehumanization. Dehumanization can lead at its most serious level to institutional neurosis. Russell Barton describes the "disease" as ". . . characterized by apathy, lack of initiative, loss of interest more marked in things and events not immediately personal or present, submissiveness, and sometimes no expression of feelings of resentment at harsh or unfair orders. There is also . . . a resigned acceptance that things will go on as they are—unchangingly, inevitably, and indefinitely."

Institutional neurotics become so adapted to the institutional environment that they give up a desire to rejoin the insecurity of the outside world. If released, they cause themselves to be returned.

How institutions can become agents of pseudo-choice to the extent that they contribute to the problem they exist to solve can be seen by a look at specific institutions—prisons, asylums and schools.

PRISONS AND JAILS

In eighteenth-century United States, there existed a wide range of punishments for criminal offenses—fines, whipping, the stocks, banishment. A sentence of imprisonment was uncommon and never used alone. Local jails were used for men in the process of judgment and they very much resembled regular homes. They had heavy-duty doors and locks but their design was the same as for an ordinary residence. The keeper and his family lived in the jail, occupying rooms little different from those assigned to the prisoners. Calvinist doctrines held sway at the time and they stressed the depravity of man and the cunning of the devil, conditions that jails would do little to overcome.

Around 1800, laws were reformed and Calvinism gradually gave way to the imported Enlightenment. Prisons were established not as correctional institutions but as a form of punishment more humane than hanging and less brutal than whipping. By the 1820s, Americans were convinced that the family environment was the key factor in producing criminals. Penitentiaries were founded based on the idea that isolation and a regular discipline would correct the deviant. The prison would remove the offender from temptation. Since a bad environment had led the criminal to evil, this new surrounding would lead him out of crime.

The idea that a strict discipline removed from "the world" would cause personal reform gave way to the idea that punishment would deter antisocial behavior. The mistakenness of this basic idea has long been obvious but institutions resist change tenaciously, and prisons are no exception.

Since 1967, there have been four presidential commissions and over five hundred books and articles pleading for prison reform. But since prisons have become an institution, they staunchly remain in existence in spite of abundant evidence that they cause positive harm to society.

The 4037 jails in this country have conditions as bad as prisons even though 52 percent of those behind bars have not yet been convicted of any crime. In the Colonies they would have been living with a family or in a simple, state-supported boardinghouse instead of enduring punishment and dehumanization. Forty percent of all released inmates (75 percent in some areas) are returned to prison within five years, often for a more serious offense; 80 percent of all felonies are committed by repeaters. *Time* magazine remarked, "Something is clearly wrong with a system that spends $1 billion a year to produce a failure record that would sink any business in a month." Prisons spend an unduly large percentage of money for buildings, as is true of many institutions. According to former Attorney General Ramsey Clark, "Ninety-five percent of all the expenditures in the entire field of corrections in this country goes for custody—iron bars, stone walls, guards. Five percent goes for health services, education, developing employment skills—for hope."

Prisons and jails have become synonymous with punishment, a long way from their original intent of holding the prisoner for judgment or protecting society. America today has few "correctional institutions," only punishment institutions that turn nonconformists into hardened criminals as often as they protect society.

ALTERNATIVES TO PRISON

Looking for alternatives to prison is like searching for nonmilitary ways to fight a war. Prisons are an expression of our value system and beliefs about human nature. Usually a change in these values must precede any significant adoption of alternatives. Some possibilities to consider would include:

1. *Probation*—used rather sparingly now.
2. *Supervised restitution*—an old idea rarely used even where restitution is easy. The procedure could be similar to a lawsuit.
3. *Exile or voluntary banishment*—the prisoners of Attica asked to be provided with transportation to a noncapitalist country. Could one-way tickets be granted to those who wanted them and who could find a country to accept them?
4. *Law reform*—crime is defined in such a way as to punish the poor and reward the rich and powerful. No prison reform could be truly effective without law reform also.
5. *Drug control*—*Brave New World* has its soma; perhaps some form of nonaggression pill could be used.
6. *Medical control*—if the theory that antisocial behavior is caused by genetic inheritance is ever accepted, the natural implication is that surgery could cure the problem. Brain surgery?
7. *Penal colony*—Tres Marias Island serves as a penal colony for Mexico. It is over thirty thousand acres where criminals with long records are sent. They can work farms or businesses on the nearly self-contained island. They can marry and be joined by their families to live on the island. Once a month they don prison garb and are counted.
8. *Halfway houses*—drug-treatment centers might serve as a model for personal rehabilitation.

ASYLUMS AND MENTAL HOSPITALS

In the early Colonies, insanity was believed to be more or less a result of God's will and the work of the devil. By the pre-Civil War era, doctors agreed that insanity was a physical disease of the brain. But what caused the disease? The common opinion, voiced to the point of cliché, was that insanity is a price to be paid for civilization.

Finally insanity, like crime, was viewed as the result of a poor environment. Therefore, if the insane could be given a new atmosphere, they could be cured. So by 1850, almost every Northeastern and Midwestern legislature supported an asylum. By 1860, twenty-eight of the thirty-three states had public institutions for the "insane."

Medical superintendents at these institutions located the roots of the problem in the fluid and changing quality of American life as compared to the more stable European ways. Therefore, the institution provided order and routine as a cure. The common belief at the time was that the asylum would not only cure the insane, but also provide the rest of society with a model of healthy living. There was a Utopian spirit about both early asylums and prisons. The charge of both institutions was to bring order to the victims of a disorganized society.

For at least fifteen years misleading statistics helped the general public believe the asylums worked miracles. For example, at Pennsylvania's Friends' asylum 87 persons accounted for 274 recoveries. A single patient admitted, discharged and readmitted five times meant five "cures." Using this method of evaluation, cures were consistently near the 100 percent figure.

Gradually the nature of the asylums changed to a sort of prison for those whose behavior is definitely unacceptable but not criminal. The "nut house" was viewed with fear and served to hide the problem of mental illness and provide a false sense of security.

Today we live in a society where more people lose their freedom through imprisonment in a "mental hospital" than in penal institutions. In 1964 (and the figures have not changed significantly in ratio since then) on any given day there were 563,354 people in hospitals for mental diseases and 186,735 in institutions for the mentally retarded. That same year there were 214,356 in Federal and state prisons.

The number in prisons voluntarily was, naturally, near zero. But, surprisingly, of the number committed to mental institutions only at the most 10 percent were there voluntarily. In most states, physicians have the power to place a person in a mental hospital for as long as fifteen days without any kind of court order. With a court order (which is often a mere formality) a person may be imprisoned for life in a mental hospital.

Many in mental hospitals need some form of help but the subjection to the dehumanizing aspects of the total institution eventually leads them to escape responsibility through institutional neurosis. They adapt to the expectations of others and actually find in their "craziness" a new power. The drugs used as part of the treatment often serve to hide the problem from the patient, and decline in mental health is viewed as a sign that more drugs and commitment and tests are needed, all of which tend to aggravate the problem.

Horror stories of conditions in asylums are common. A seventeen-year-old boy in New York voluntarily committed himself to a mental hospital because of what he called "chronic depression and compulsive thoughts of suicide since the age of thirteen." He was charged $60 a day and for the first four days neither spoke to a nurse or doctor. A five-minute conference with a doctor on the fifth day was of no help. His room contained three other patients, and had a strong overhead light which stayed on all night. A fainting spell in the corridor left him crumpled on the floor overnight, completely escaping the attention of anyone on the staff. After thirteen days and heated arguments, he was allowed to leave and seek help elsewhere.

MENTAL INSTITUTIONS: ALTERNATIVES

Dr. Thomas Szasz is well worth study. He claims very simply and radically that there is no such thing as "mental illness." The mind is not an organ or part of the body. Therefore, it cannot be diseased in the same sense as the body can. The term mental illness is not a reality but a metaphor. A more obvious example of this acceptance of a metaphor for reality is found in the expression "nervous breakdown." People generally accept this as an event that happens to people. In reality, nerves don't break down. The word is a metaphor and euphemism for an occurrence that medical science cannot yet understand.

Szasz compares our belief in mental illness with the medieval belief in witchcraft. In his book, *The Manufacture of Madness*, he presents parallels between the two that are genuinely frightening. He sees mental hospitals as a way society uses to control behavior even though it harms the individual. Those who bother society without strictly breaking a law (those who do break a law go to prison) can be removed by being stigmatized as "crazy" and locked up in a prison called a "mental hospital."

To Szasz, involuntary mental hospitalization must be abolished completely. Talk of reforming mental hospitals is equivalent to talk of better ways of slavery or burning witches; they are in need of abolition and not reform.

Another "alternative" approach is that of R. D. Laing, who has attracted a growing number of radical followers. His belief is that insanity is a trip to be gone through with a great potential for human growth rather than one to be avoided with drugs and straitjackets. In his book, *The Politics of Experience*, he says concerning insanity, "Can we not see that this voyage is not what we need to be cured of, but that it is itself a natural way of healing our own appalling state of alienation called normality?" His idea of treating insanity involves guidance of "patients" through their trips into inner space by people who have already been there and back again.

SCHOOLS

Schools are not "total institutions" in the strict sense of the phrase. Students do go home every day and have a substantial number of nonschool days during the year. But since most children in the nation attend school for about thirteen thousand hours by the time they are seventeen, the institution of school has much in common with total institutions such as orphanages, jails, the military and asylums. The fact that almost everyone in the nation spends so many thousands of hours of a lifetime in schools makes them the most "total" institution of all when viewed in terms of effects on society.

School is the only universal institution, the only one not requiring a person to be ill, criminal, insane or possessive of some other deviant trait in order to be institutionalized. Schools exist to socialize young people, to train them to accept a certain type of ordered existence. A common misconception about schools is that they are primarily for the education of students. But our states have no compulsory education laws, only compulsory schooling.

The first compulsory attendance law was passed in Massachusetts in 1852, and by 1918 every state had a compulsory attendance law. In the 1950s, Virginia, Mississippi and South Carolina repealed theirs in order to circumvent Federally ordered integration. The right of the state to order young people to school has been challenged and upheld in the courts. The reasoning behind the court decisions is not that a democracy needs an educated electorate (that was Thomas Jefferson's political rhetoric, not a court recognizing realities), but that the citizens of the nation need schools to serve as a security against crime, misery, loss of property and disregard for law and order. In other words, schools exist to protect the rest of us from a world in which kids are turned loose every day. Laws do not require schools to educate, they simply require students to be physically present rather than in the job market or roaming the streets.

The function of schooling in our society is to take young humans with an almost unlimited capacity to become an astonishing variety of adults and shape them into those possibilities that are socially acceptable. Schools exist to limit human possibilities. The institution of schooling in a society of cannibals would exist to teach young people to be good cannibals. Presumably, home-economics class in such a society would be vastly different from the same subject matter taught in the United States. But in both cases, the teachers are very likely altruistic individuals who wish to help. In both cases the school is socializing the students—teaching values and beliefs proper to current society. If a student would pass through school in the cannibal society and graduate not convinced of the rightness of eating other people, he or she might be branded a failure. If a large number of students would fail to accept cannibalism, the school system itself might be branded a failure and the elders would call for drastic reforms.

The curriculum, the list of subjects taught in American schools leads one to believe that history, math, English and science are the prime lessons taught. But the subject matter taught is secondary to the process of schooling. Students must learn to follow directions, take orders, respect older people, do assignments on time, learn an acceptable concept of neatness and observe various written and unwritten rules of decorum. Their ability to master these social skills usually determines the painfulness of their progression through the schooling system.

If education were the prime concern of the state, then laws would require that students be able to meet certain standards of learning rather than subject themselves to a near total institution for a period of years. State laws define schooling in terms of attendance for a specified number of hours per day and days per year.

Teachers and administrators do not consider themselves society's baby-sitters or stabilizers of the job marketplace. They think of themselves, and attempt to act, as educators. Much of their frustration comes from the conflict between themselves as human beings desiring to educate other human beings and the existence of an institutional setting in which students view themselves as prisoners. The conflict is between schools and education. For schools to offer truly effective education, they need to be deinstitutionalized. But before schools can be deinstitutionalized, society has to agree on activities that young people can take part in during the day (socially valuable work, apprenticeships, etc.) that will benefit both them and society. Until such reforms take place, schools will continue to be battlegrounds between the teachers and administrators who wish to help and the institution that aims to control and socialize.

School as a total institution can be clearly seen by pointing out the comparisons between schools and prisons as institutions. This is not to say that schools *are* prisons, although both institutions do have the confinement of people to keep them "off the streets" as one objective. The following is a very incomplete list of similarities between most prisons and most schools:

- A small number of people (teachers, guards) are faced with the control of a larger number (students, prisoners).
- The clientele of neither institution is there by free choice.

Students past the age of compulsory attendance are an exception to this rule—college is an exception for most students.

- The buildings of both institutions are similar in appearance. Both are designed and furnished for ease of maintenance, resistance to vandalism and theft and crowd control. Long corridors and a general lack of color often prevail.

- The clock and the calendar are the prime instruments for determining the length of stay of the clients. Both students and prisoners can sometimes leave the institution early, but these are exceptions.

- Movement during the day is tightly restricted and governed by carefully measured time periods. Clients are required to be in a certain place at a certain time. Eating, going to the bathroom and other ordinary functions become problematic.

- Drugs and discipline are a major problem. Sometimes drugs are used to control inmates. Tranquilizers are used in prisons (and mental hospitals) and drugs such as Ritalin in schools.

- Both have hall guards and places that are off limits. Visitors to both institutions often are required to obtain a pass allowing access to the interior of the building.

- Both prisoners and students are offered a minimum of choices about what happens to them during the day. Both institutions have a form of puppet government that is strictly controlled by the administration. Both (sometimes) have an inmate-controlled press that is subject to censorship.

- Physical appearance such as clothing (even uniforms) and hair length is regulated sometimes to extremes. This tendency was more common in previous years.

- Both institutions have a series of special privileges that the guards or teachers can offer to students. In both cases, these are used as a source of control or discipline.

This incomplete list is not offered here to convince readers that schools are evil places like jail—although some of them are. It exists to point out the fact that schools share characteristics with all institutions. Once this is recognized, then problems that these characteristics cause can be dealt with as institutional problems. Many attempts to deal with problems in schools (and other institutions) deal only in pseudo-choice and partial solutions. They attempt to find better ways to change flat tires or offer motorists the courtesy of free coffee while their car is repaired.

It is outside the scope of this slim volume to suggest solutions to complex social problems. But hopefully this chapter will help alert responsible individuals to the presence of pseudo-choice in dealing with these problems. Problems in our social institutions might often require deinstitutionalizing in order to produce a truly lasting solution. As long as that truck is allowed to scatter nails every morning, any other solution will be based on pseudo-choice.

Chapter 7
Mythology Today

"Daddy, where does the moon go in the morning?" my inquisitive daughter asks one clear autumn night. I begin my explanation feeling fatherly pride at knowing the mysteries of the universe. I talk about planets and revolutions, about racing through space at thousands of miles an hour and about reflections from the sun. There are a few gaps left by the fading memory of my high-school general science course, but the answer seems basically sound. Christine says "oh" and moves away to play with something more interesting—a pile of leaves.

Reflecting on the question I realize my answer was a scientific one, admittedly weak but still built on the assumptions and thought patterns of human-as-scientist. I realize that in all of human history this scene must have been repeated millions of times and that I, unlike my predecessors, am unique in my total reliance upon science to provide answers. My ancestors saw the moon as a key to the meaning of life, as a part of the myth that explained the world. But I am the victim of science texts, NASA and televised moon landings sponsored by Tang. The symbol of the end of the common man as mythmaker was the landing of the fragile, windowed womb of the Apollo space capsule on the moon.

In the space capsule, ironically named for the Greek twin of moon goddess Diana, myth and science intersected. When humans plodded around clumsily, swung a golf club, hacked away at rocks and planted a national symbol, the sacred cathedral of the sky was profaned finally and forever. The magical, mythical moon became a hunk of ashen rock. There are no more mysteries up there and so there will be no more myths.

The moon as a cycle in nature is no more. Even Darwin believed that since man originated in the watery depths so much influenced by the moon, its cycles and irregularities were imprinted indelibly upon us. The moon's irregularity gave us lunatics as a name for those who acted unpredictably. The word menstruation comes from the same root as month and moon, all meaning "to measure." As recently as 1937, researchers surveyed ten thousand women to determine that menstruation was not somehow controlled by the cycles of the moon.

The nation was secretly disappointed when the men from earth walked around the moon and failed to discover a man in the moon. Back in 1969 we watched TV screens and held our breaths, hoping maybe some otherworldly moon creature would scuttle from behind a rock and change the course of human history. We were prepared for anything, but were given nothing. Technology had replaced myth and mystery.

When my daughter asked her question, I never considered that the moon embodies the universal law of becoming—of birth and death. The moon, like man, is subject to birth and death and embodies the constant hope for a rebirth. Our autumnal holidays and Easter are dated by the appearance of the moon but few notice its presence. For centuries, festivals of the new moon were celebrated by peoples to welcome the reappearance of the extinguished light in the sky.

But all this richness of meaning is lost now. Perhaps my daughter would have listened longer to a spinner of mythic tales from the past capable of wondrous moon stories. Perhaps she would learn more about life from them than from even the best of scientists.

Myths today are considered as something-people-did-long-ago-before-they-knew-any-better. Students traditionally study a limited number of Greek and Roman myths and are later tested on who is related to whom and who did what. Seldom are we taught to develop our own ability to create myths—to become mythmakers. And so we have lost the mindset that led the ancients to look into a night sky and see all of history and life written in its lights.

In fact, large cities are star stealers. It has been at least a dozen years since I have had the privilege to see a clear night sky with its infinitude of lights. The universe as seen at night from the isolation of northern Wisconsin or the Texas hill country far from big cities is a sight that fewer and fewer Americans are privileged to behold. To see such a sky is to realize the universe and one's own place. But the cities have stolen this experience just as science has stolen the impetus to create myths. We settle, instead, for light shows at rock concerts for a $7.50 ticket or the glitter of Times Square or the safety of streetlights that protect us from prowlers and turn the skin purple.

One of our inheritances from the Victorian age was the enthronement of the rational. And we have yet to recover from the Victorian concept of myth as fiction. Book titles such as *Foreign Policy: The Myth and the Reality* or *The Myth of Social Security* tend to perpetuate this concept. Only recently have we begun to rediscover that rational thought and science are only a limited approach to reality—the irrational and the mythic are making a comeback.

But thwarting the rediscovery of the value of myth is the same snake in the American Garden that is found with television, food, transportation and leisure—corporate control and pseudo-choice. We are content to entrust mythmaking to the corporations that control entertainment and mass media.

Entertainment is not an area of life subject to the laws of pseudo-choice. No conglomerate controls the choice of activities we engage in to entertain ourselves actively. A few entertainment areas, tourism and the family vacation for one, are rapidly coming under the influence of pseudo-choice. We saw in the food chapter that restaurants are succumbing to the temptation to serve frozen prepared dinners offered by the largest food processors, but it is still possible to eat a delicious, real-food dinner away from home.

The segment of the realm of entertainment that has come most under the influence of pseudo-choice is the mythic dimension. Much of what we do in the name of play and entertainment is a way of sharing in and affirming the values and beliefs of society. The myths offered for our participation are no longer created by the cooperation of generations passing down ancient stories and re-creating them in the process. Myth lives in any culture in the activities of its people. In twentieth-century America, it is very much alive in film, television and popular spectator sports. Those who find this idea surprising are those who define myth only in terms of ancient fictions used only to fill time in school or provide copy for $25 coffee table encyclopedias.

Myth experts Robert Graves and Raphael Patai once agreed upon a definition of myth as ". . . dramatic stories that form a sacred charter either authorizing the continuance of ancient institutions, customs, rites and beliefs in the area where they are current, or approving alterations." Critic Mark Schorer describes a myth as ". . . a large, controlling image that gives philosophical meaning to the facts of ordinary life." Films and television series serve as the mass creators of myths. The most popular films and TV shows are those whose mythmaking creators have managed to capture some powerful means of affirming popular values (customs, rites, beliefs) or approving changes in traditional values.

We saw earlier that soap operas affirm that happiness is possible right here on this earth for those who believe in it and keep trying. The long-popular quiz shows embody the myth of instant riches that viewers can experience vicariously. The genie who would grant three wishes is replaced by a TV emcee with wads of hundred-dollar bills to distribute to the studio audience.

The situation comedy (represented by series such as "I Love Lucy," "Bewitched," "Beverly Hillbillies," "That Girl") is one genre of television that has mythic proportions. The sitcom, according to Horace Newcomb in his book, *T.V.: The Most Popular Art*, has a distinct structure with four basic parts: ". . . the establishment of the situation, the complication, the confusion that ensues, and the alleviation of the complication." The sitcom revels in confusion caused by human error or misunderstandings. The fact that the characters are "unreal" or out of touch with everyday life is unimportant. The key to the sitcom is that everything comes out all right. Each episode is a reaffirmation in mythic dimensions of the belief that everything comes out all right in the end and problems can be solved quickly and completely. The sitcom genre became almost a lost art after the days of "I Love Lucy," but new programs under consideration as replacements for the ratings losers of the 1975-76 season include a whopping 44 percent in the situation comedy classification. A revival in situation comedies indicates a social need to be reminded that in the midst of problems everything will work out all right. Perhaps we have passed through the era of needing to realize mythically that law and order always wins out to needing a sign of hope for everyday problems.

Domestic comedies (from "Father Knows Best" to the Mary Tyler Moore Productions to "Maude" and "All in the Family") tend to work within the mythic confines of middle-class values (even when they deal with upper- or lower-class characters). They reaffirm the family as a sheltering unit within which problems are solved.

"Mission Impossible" was a very popular TV series and its reruns remain one of the most watched syndicated series. The show was popular partly because it was well scripted and directed, but also because it embodied certain cultural values that needed mythification at the time. The series affirmed that there were evil people "out there" who would stop at nothing to subvert American values. Viewers learned that espionage was a force for good. The "Mission Impossible" team often went to assist in the "overthrow" of some foreign strong-man dictator and restore the rule of the country to the "good guy" who would restore a democratic process.

The show helped affirm the need for American intervention in foreign affairs and taught that the United States always sides with good in the overthrow of evil. The Impossible Mission of the United States was the maintenance of world peace and goodness. History has since shown that the real-world counterparts of the Impossible Mission force lived in a less black and white world, but myth is not history. The series also helped perpetuate belief in the power of a well-run organization with the magic of technology to achieve any goal it set out to do without the use of violence.

"Mission Impossible," like many other TV series, was more

than mere entertainment. It also served to teach and remind viewers of the American Mission and our place in the world.

The fact that the source of these mythic forms of entertainment watched by millions is limited to the three networks places them securely in the realm of pseudo-choice. A study of network diversity from 1953 to 1974 was conducted by Joseph Dominick and Millard Pearce of the University of Georgia. The study reveals that since 1957, action/adventure shows have dominated network offerings to the extent that ". . . for the last 17 years, the most prevalent influence on audiences of prime-time television may be reality as portrayed in the world of the action/adventure series." The study also supports the relation between pseudo-choice and a lack of diversity. The study shows a nearly consistent decline in the diversity of types of programs offered since 1953. More and more program time is devoted to fewer and fewer program types. Dominick and Pearce echo the theme of this book by concluding that ". . . such a decline represents fewer and fewer choices available to the audience and indicates that network attention is being focused on fewer and fewer topics."

ABC, CBS and NBC (with generous support from UPI and AP) are the nation's prime mythmakers. The characters they create by magically rearranged phosphor on the TV screen are as real as the Greek gods once were. In the submythic world of soap operas, the degree of viewer identification with characters is amazing. Some years ago, an actor who played a villainous character on "Secret Storm" was reportedly shot by a viewer. Eileen Fulton, who played the much hated "Lisa" on "As the World Turns," was hit by an angry woman who called her a "terrible woman." She required police protection going to and from the studio when she began to receive threats on her life in the mail.

But television cooperates with another set of mythmakers, the poets of Hollywood. In *America in the Movies*, critic Michael Wood voices the opinion that ". . . my general feeling is that films deal mainly in worries that are not so much contradictory as muddled, clumsily overlapping, unexamined. The mythological function of movies is to examine them without seeming to look at them at all. Movies assuage the discomforts of blurred minds; but they also maintain the blur. That is their business."

Any film or TV series that is immensely popular, judged even by so prosaic a means as box-office receipts or Nielsen ratings, is mythic. Film scholar Stuart Kaminsky points out that American filmgoers have divided films into two kinds—entertainments and "serious films." "Entertainment only" films are generally panned or ignored by the critics but draw people out of their houses and into the mythic space and time of a movie theater. Serious films are written about in great length by critics and often play only to small audiences in large cities. This turn of events simply acts to confirm the critics' determination to work ever harder to educate the film-going public to appreciate "better" films. Film teachers in high schools and colleges are guilty of the same distinction and currently threaten to turn film into an art form as popular as poetry or basket weaving. As critic Pauline Kael observed, "If you don't think the movies can be killed, you underestimate the power of education.

Kaminsky, in an article in *Take One* magazine, treats this distinction between mere entertainment and serious art with suspicion. He says that ". . . the first thing to be understood is that if we and millions of others respond to a film, then that film is worth understanding and is saying something very meaningful to us." He does not refer to popular films as mythic, but he does point out that *The Poseidon Adventure* (a box-office blockbluster apparently enjoyed by the whole nation minus a few film critics) is a reverse Dante's *Inferno*, an ascent from hell to salvation led by Gene Hackman as a contemporary Messiah.

So-called "disaster films," such as *The Poseidon Adventure*, enjoyed a brief period of box-office euphoria not because America needed to watch disasters, but because the mythmakers provided realistic imaginary disasters and believable Messiahs. The shark in *Jaws* was certainly the film's leading character, but people flocked to the film in order to feel relieved and breathe easily that a hero conquered the beast with good old-fashioned courage (and a bit of luck).

One form of popular film that has survived the test of time (making it even more universal as a mythic form) is the monster movie. *King Kong* has survived since 1933 (and revised in 1976) and still attacks the Empire State Building every week on theater screens and afternoon movies. *Kong* is more than an entertaining collection of special effects and chaotic violence. *Kong* reaffirms the ape in all of us, the hairy brute force that wants to lash out at all those forces of modern civilization that attack and pester us. In the film Kong is presented as king of his island, a noble brute coping with daily problems of dinosaurs and pterodactyls. But this innocent creature is captured by greedy men out to exploit him. He is chained and charged with earning money for a businessman. Any nine-to-fiver dissatisfied with his job in the city can see some of himself in Kong. While dreaming of an unfettered life with nature, he is bound to work every day in the big city or various local versions of the Empire State Building. King Kong embodies the repressed animal spirit condemned to live in a jungle of concrete and steel. Somewhere in the desk-chained city dweller exists the urge to swat out at the sterile architecture, the commuter trains and technology with a hairy arm and squash a few polluting but unpaid autos in the palm of a hand. The myth of the brutal but good beast within, chained by civilization, is enacted on the screen in King Kong.

Mary Shelley also presented a sympathetic monster, one who wants good, who tries to befriend children but who is destroyed by that same technology that created him. The fact that Frankenstein was written by an adolescent is significant. To understand the mythic content of monster films requires a realization that they have survived more successfully than the old gangster and musical films of the same era and that they are traditionally seen by the teenagers of each generation.

That adolescents are a major factor in the continuing resurrections of monsters is appropriate. For the central fact of adolescence is physical change that is unstoppable and unwilled. Sometimes the urges and feelings of puberty seem antisocial and place the teenager in the role of the reluctant rebel, the outsider, the misfit, neither adult nor child. Teenagers readily see themselves as monsters forced by society to conform and repress the emerging hairy ape. Love and sexuality become important but are condemned by society and are inevitably doomed. Fay Wray and Kong have no hope of moving into a suburban condominium any more than do teenage lovers no matter how pure and undying their love. Both the monster and the teenager must cope with alienation and a society unable to appreciate their goodness.

Films such as *Frankenstein*, *King Kong* or *The Poseidon Adventure* are mythic tales to twentieth-century Americans just as much as Greek and Roman myths were to the Greeks and Romans. But the choices offered are increasingly limited to accepting the myths created by one of several film studios, one of three TV networks or a few advertising agencies.

Before 1948, the motion-picture industry was dominated by Paramount, Twentieth Century-Fox, Warner Brothers, RKO and Loew's. Federal antitrust action in 1948 separated the ownership of theaters from production and distribution and prohibited many of the practices that had given the "big five" such a dominant position. But by 1972 three motion-picture studios reaped over 50 percent of all the film rental dollars in the United States and by 1975 that figure was still holding at 50 percent. The top five companies control over 70 percent of the film rental dollar. The companies with the largest share of the film rental market in 1975 were Universal with a 25 percent share, Columbia with 13 percent, Paramount with a little over 11 percent and United Artists with a 10.7 percent share.

Compared to writing a book, recording a song or producing a painting, filmmaking is expensive. But the control of production by conglomerates who turn out only million-dollar films makes the development of true art and skilled folk artists in film unlikely. The preservation and creation of myths have passed into the hands of the conglomerates.

Mythmakers are readily accepted in the worlds of film and television, but there is a form of "entertainment" that is engaged in by 99.9 percent of all Americans, yet is rarely considered as entertainment: watching TV commercials. Nowhere is the mythic mind harder at work today than in the world of advertising. The less creative admen simply borrow names from mythology to lend plebian products an aura of the divine. A glance through a listing of trademarks and brand names reads like an index to Larousse's *Encyclopedia of Mythology*—Ajax, Midas, Atlas, Hercules, Mercury, Apollo or Neptune.

But borrowing names is only the surface of modern myth. There is one particular mythic theme and structure that Madison Avenue uses often and effectively: an instant solution to a problem performed by magical means, often by a character with superhuman powers or by a potion with magic powers. The basic structure of these mythic commercials is the presentation of the problem followed quickly by its resolution.

Television critics select these commercials as prime examples of mindless advertising and the treatment of housewives (the favorite target of mythic ads) as third graders. But such criticism fails to see the profundity in these seemingly senseless ads. The ads appeal to the remnants of the desire to be a witch, alchemist or sorcerer—a wish advertising presents as attainable through the use of certain magic products.

Sometimes these minimyths borrow a character from ancient mythology. Always the name is changed, no doubt to protect the ad agency from a divinity suit. The White Knight of the Ajax commercials is a steal from medieval myth; Mr. Clean comes straight from the *Arabian Nights* and the Jolly Green Giant from European folklore where he is the benevolent patron saint of pea-pickers. Add to these the White Tornado, the Man from Glad, Wally the Janitor, Mother Nature, Adam and Eve, Brawny and others of more recent creation and you have a pantheon of divinities with powers sufficient to cause envy amid a gathering of ancient gods.

The problem the "gods" face usually involves a damsel in distress battling the presence of evil in one of its many guises: odors, pain, a dissatisfied husband, spotted dishes or any of the hundreds of life situations that pass as tragedy in the ad world.

Out of the air pops the mythic hero to the rescue. The prince charming-knight can be a real character like the Man from Glad or can be the product itself given life. The magic product is presented and it solves the problem instantly, turning the distressed damsel into a princess again. The commercial implies that the happy ending to the minidrama means that the housewife will be able to fight germs and nasty odors on her own, using the newly acquired magic potion. The housewife is given special knowledge and is now capable of waging battle in her kingdom of the kitchen with all the cunning and magic of the mythic heroes. In fact, according to the commercials, the housewife is a hero of sorts, an alchemist who turns dirty floors, dishes and clothes into shiny new ones with the aid of her magic solutions. The commercials succeed in turning housework into a task with mythic and heroic dimensions. Such mythic appeals are easily adaptable to the image of the "liberated" woman: mythic ads stress liberation through magic and instant change.

The housewife as hero with special potions given by the gods carries over into the area of personal hygiene. The ordinary TV-ad mortal is presented as a menace to society, exuding noxious odors from various parts of the body, trailing flaky dandruff, having bulges in the wrong places or not enough in the right places. In general, the commercials, using a mythic approach, present the victim as untouchable. The girls ignore him or the guys never look twice. But the Fairy Godmother and Prince Charming haven't died; they've simply gone into television advertising. Some new deodorant, soap, perfume or hair spray will turn the ugly into a ravishing beauty.

In these commercials for personal care products the element of the miraculous conversion is what is mythic. The miracle is the difference between the before and after; the ordinary mortal is raised to a new level by the magic products. The typical thirty-second TV spot reinforces the idea of the product as providing an *instant* solution. Such changes take on the character of a magic metamorphosis as convincing and dramatic as the change from frog to prince.

The use of mythic devices as the *deus ex machina* solution and the magic metamorphosis is not mere coincidence nor is it a stretching of an overworked literary imagination. The magical solution of problems or magic conversion is a common facet of myth for exactly the same reason as it is common in TV commercials. Such solutions and changes remain a universal wish. Who doesn't wish to be able to work magic in some area of life or be able to perform some magic plastic surgery on oneself? Myths animate these desires and commercials capitalize on them.

During childhood the imagination is fed stories of giants and strange magic creatures. To a three-foot-tall child the whole world of adults fits nicely into this magic world. A child begins in a world of magic and gradually grows out of it. But the childhood belief in miracles and benevolent or evil supercreatures remains. It is this remnant of belief in the magical and mythical worlds that is tapped in television commercials. If science can invent "instant" coffee, tea and angel food cake, why not instant popularity, status and complete power? To ask, "But does anyone really believe those dumb commercials?" is certainly to miss their deep appeal. As we have seen earlier, the mistaken belief in personal immunity allows the magic of the ad to work. The use of mythic elements directs attention away from a rational product choice and into the world of pseudo-choice.

Since sport is still a mythic world, it is only natural that those who excel in this world be used by Madison Avenue to lend some of their godlike aura to corporate products. Sport's pantheon is enshrined in various halls of fame. Its heroes and gods are described by sportscasters in superhuman terms as people possessing magical powers. The star athlete is looked upon with awe and is, in the eye of his worshipers, the closest thing to a god on earth in this secular society. His handwriting is a treasured object, to have spoken to such a demigod is to have been in the presence of the divinity and lived to tell others. The heroes are crushing, super-fast, powerful, crafty, intelligent, brutal, sometimes handsome and mean. What more could one ask of a god?

Since these athlete heroes are gods and come from the world of myth, they are prime targets to "endorse" products. So Joe Namath, O. J. Simpson, or older heroes like Mickey Mantle and Joe DiMaggio and dozens of others are likely to appear on television using various products. The idea behind these ads is not to convince the viewer that because Muhammad Ali uses Brut, he should too, or that if you use Brut, kid, you will someday be a famous and wealthy world champion (although they work on this level at times with fans and children who identify closely enough with the athlete). The hero endorsements say simply that the product endorsed belongs in the superhuman world of the gods. Once the media have established divinity for an individual, any-thing he or she associates with is given a touch of the divine glow. Certain candy bars or cola drinks become "food of the gods." By drinking or eating them, a bit of divinity rubs off on the ordinary mortal, thus satisfying slightly his or her own drive toward divinity and immortality. The ads create an allusion of participating, ever so slightly, in a world one can never hope to attain, an ordered world that is perfect and is peopled by superhuman, godlike beings.

The force behind hero endorsements is the same as the ancient belief that whatever is touched by a god receives some manna (power) from the contact. Religions still preserve the ritual importance of the touch or the laying on of hands as a remnant of this belief. The sometimes frantic desire for a relic, either of a religious saint or secular hero, is another sign that people still believe whatever a "great one" touches is itself elevated to a new level. The old woman in the back of a church worshiping a bone fragment of some long-dead saint and the ecstatic teenybopper who has just torn the shirt off a pop hero both believe in this magic transfer of power.

Not only sports heroes, but also cultural gods such as the stars of "stage and screen," the handsome men and their mysterious women, sometimes endorse products. Currently the only "stars" seen on television seem to be those past their "divine" prime who are otherwise out of work and need the residuals to cushion their retirement. If only Madison Avenue could collar Mick Jagger for Mennen Skin Bracer, Paul Newman for Suzuki, Carly Simon and James Taylor for First Federal Savings, or maybe Jane Fonda for Levi's. But the superstars of the highest order have learned that by imitating the well-established, cultural pattern of the "myth of the absent god," their divinity is enhanced.

Some heroes are still inaccessible to the ad and talent agencies, perhaps as befits true gods. So the creation of magical items out of the ordinary products of Lever Brothers and Procter & Gamble will continue with fictional gods; mythic ads continue because they sell soap. And they sell soap because there is in us all a part that still believes in myth and magic. In ancient cultures heroes were a dime a dozen; today they are about $25,000 a minute.

The heroic figure comes to us straight from mythology and, in spite of talk about the death of the hero, is alive and well in contemporary life. Mythologists have found that hero stories fit a very definite pattern in many cultures. The pattern they find is that of a superhuman or divine being who sets out into the land of evil to battle courageously with the enemy, be it dragons, beasts, a magical creature or even other gods. This character is threatened and tested severely and faces seemingly impossible tasks. But he struggles and wins, defeating the enemy and often gaining some valuable possession which he brings back to the forces of goodness. Hercules fits this pattern as well as Superman and so do most modern heroes. Both entertainment and news media define and create our heroes.

Take almost any film or television series involving a hero and apply the mythic formula. In the now syndicated TV series "Mission Impossible," the hero is a team. The evil forces are usually villains of the underworld. The word "underworld" is a revealing choice, showing a direct link to ancient myth. The IM force represents goodness and battles the underworld exactly as in ancient myth. In reality the IM force seems to be patterned loosely after quasi-legal CIA agents. The series has been banned in some foreign countries because of its negative presentation of foreign governments.

The Impossible Mission force has no supernatural powers as did mythical heroes. Instead they use technology to achieve almost magical or miraculous effects. They battle the evil ones, are invariably victorious, take considerable risk and undergo constant narrow escapes while remaining virtuous and seemingly indestructible. Exactly like the mythic heroes who preceded them.

The mythic hero in ancient times was Samson, Hercules, Zeus or Atlas. Today he is Captain Kirk, Kung Fu, Ironside, James Bond or Billy Jack. All these figures have extraordinary abilities and all risk their lives to battle evil forces and bestow favors on mankind. One current trend in today's heroes is to rely less on their individuality and more on their membership in a team or group. This is culturally valuable since most socially valued work is now done in teams, panels, groups or task forces. It is also fashionable to endow the hero with some quasi-magical trappings of science.

Everyone identifies to some extent with a person he or she views as heroic. The hero evokes that part of us that would like to be brave, a symbol of goodness, powerful, worshiped and popular. Thus, Superman is a perfect hero type. The mild-mannered Clark

Kent is more like what we are in reality. But underneath this tame exterior is the mighty superbeing. Clark Kent is what we know we are; Superman is what we dream we can become. Because Superman reflects a wish fulfillment of our culture, he has remained a popular hero, elevated even to the seventh heaven of a television serial and a feature film.

In fact, every hero, real or fictional, mirrors the time and place in which he or she lives. The hero is a public reflection of humanity's innermost hopes and beliefs. This helps explain why certain public figures become heroes of mythic proportions while others, just as capable and perhaps even more effective, are relegated to the public doghouse or at best to neglect.

In Lord Raglan's classic 1936 work, *The Hero: A Study in Tradition, Myth, and Drama,* he names twenty-two elements that seem part of the heroic saga. Heroes like Oedipus, Theseus, Moses, Christ and King Arthur are rooted more in their sharing of the heroic saga than in their historical records. Marshall Fishwick in *The Hero, American Style* applies Raglan's theory to the most recent heroic American President, John F. Kennedy, to show how his now mythic fame fits the ancient structure:

> *His father was called to a royal court (as Ambassador to the Court of Saint James's) and the son was educated by (presumably) wise men (at Harvard). Then he went off to fight an evil dragon (the Japanese Navy) and after a bloody fracas (PT 109) triumphed and returned to marry the beautiful princess (Jackie). Having inherited his father's kingdom (politics) he fought and defeated a second contender (Nixon) before taking over as ruler (President). For a time he reigned smoothly and prescribed laws. Then he suddenly lost favor (Bay of Pigs), tried to rally his people, and died a sudden and mysterious death (did Oswald really shoot Kennedy?). Amid great mourning (the first worldwide television funeral) he was buried on a sacred hillside (Arlington). Now he has many shrines (a cultural center, airport, library, highway and space launching site).*

So whomever a person or culture chooses as hero indicates what that person or culture values. The gushing, sentimental hero of

Victorian times was replaced in more mechanized worlds by the coolness of a Billy the Kid, James Bond or Bonnie and Clyde.

Heroes have recently fallen upon bad times. Outside the world of athletics and entertainment, heroes seem few and far between. Every culture needs heroes even if their creation takes a little bending of history. Out of the age of the antihero certainly will rise a new pack of heroes and gods. They are probably around right now merely waiting elevation from the media and popular tastes. But whoever they might be, it is assured they will be created and offered for consumption by a handful of mythmakers.

RECORDS AND RADIO

For centuries, music has played an important role in the structure of cultures and in the communication of the society's myths, values and traditions. Today music has become an industry dominated by records and radio.

Anthropologists have often observed that modern Western society is nearly unique in the history of civilizations in its absence of clearly defined rites of passage to adulthood. The myths and rituals of earlier cultures have vanished in the United States, leading to adolescence as a troubled period of too-old-to-be-a-child-and-too-young-to-be-an-adult. But the record/TV industry assumes its role as cultural provider and gives young girls the phenomenon of "teen idols" as rites of passage.

Girls age nine to twelve buy most of the singles sold in the United States. During this age, the girls often adopt a "teen idol" to help ease themselves through puberty. Once they become old enough to go on dates, they lose interest in the idols, who fade away only to be replaced by new ones for the new generation of nine- to twelve-year-olds. The idols have images carefully controlled by managers so that they serve as "paramours in absentia," as love objects to fill the gap between the teddy bear and the local quarterback. As once-teen-idol Bobby Sherman explained, "I'm part of the process of becoming mature for these girls."

The teen idols appeal, as one *TV Guide* writer aptly noted, ". . . to that twilight zone between childhood and maturity when girls from 6 to 16 start to become interested in boys but don't know why. His youthful idolators are reaching out for a shy, good-looking boy who sings about puppy love and acceptance, who gyrates in a manner that is 'groovy' but is not overtly sexy."

From Eddie Fisher to Ricky Nelson, Fabian, the Beatles, the Monkees, Bobby Sherman, David Cassidy and Donny Osmond to whoever reigns today, the teen idols are not artists of song or the recording arts, although some of them have considerable talent. They are the answer of entertainment moguls to the need for a rite of passage for girls. Conveniently, the idols turn into a big business, grossing millions of dollars during their necessarily short-lived careers. Teenyboppers have the pseudo-choice of spending $35 million for Bobby Sherman love objects or David Cassidy artifacts.

Year after year a mere five record companies account for over 55 percent of the records that sell in any significant number, and the sale of phonograph records is a billion-dollar-a-year industry. It is safe to predict that next year high-school and college students (the largest buyers of records) will spend millions of dollars to purchase the produce of CBS Records (Columbia and Epic labels), RCA, Warner Communications (Warner/Reprise, Elektra, Atlantic), Capitol and MCA Records. All are conglomerates in the business of myth- and hero-making. The choice left to listeners is among whatever the leading corporations preselect. There is no effective distribution system for a wide variety of music beyond that offered by the large recording companies.

Richard Peterson and David Berger of Vanderbilt and Temple universities, respectively, studied the record industry from 1948 to 1973 and found a cyclical pattern of concentration, competition and back to concentration.

Between 1948 and 1955, RCA, Columbia, Decca and Capitol controlled the recording industry effectively through corporate controls of radio and film production companies as well as wholesale distributors, warehouses and record jobbers. The repertoire featured a handful of sure-hit recording artists and a limited number of acceptable themes. But the concentration led to a stultification and lack of variety to the extent of putting out four versions of the same hit song.

Customers finally were able to exercise some power over the concentrated industry and discovered jazz, country and western and finally rock music. The big four missed the boat on rock which they believed a passing fad, and so the big eight was born. The large companies realized the need for greater diversity in their musical offerings. They learned their lesson so that today a handful of corporate pockets accounts for most of the profits in the recording industry. A handful of "stars" also reap the majority of money that is filtered through the companies to the musicians and singers.

Peterson and Berger see the industry structure today as ". . . approaching the conditions of 1948." They speculate that as fewer controlling companies have to compete less for the entertainment dollar, the resulting product might become less diverse and rely increasingly on big names.

Popular music consists almost entirely of songs that can fit on a 45 rpm record, the length of the songs controlled by the length of time that is physically correct and timely for a jukebox. Even long-playing albums are still routinely made up of a collection of three-minute songs. This is less true today than ten years ago, but the jukebox mentality and its concomitant extra profits still give music buyers choices very much restricted to the three-minute song. Artists who wish to be "true to their music" find the limitation a distinct handicap.

Records and radio go hand in hand as partners in music and merchandising. What is played on radio determines what records sell, what is ignored by radio is very likely to be ignored in the record stores. In an unpublished manuscript on "The Structure of the Popular Music Industry," Paul Hirsch of the Sociology Department at the University of Michigan surveyed 250 college and university bookstores that sell records. He found ". . . the growing number of chart acts indicates that within ivy-thatched communities, young people's tastes correspond to those acts gaining the strongest radio exposure. The market for esoteric performers seems to be dwindling." Popular music radio stations are the electronic pipers who call the tunes that send the record buyers in search of a particular song, album or star.

The most successful radio stations in recent years have been those that adopted what was once called the "Top 40" format. The brief history of Top 40 is itself a study in progressive pseudo-choice. Top 40 was a programming innovation in the early 1950s, in response to competition from television. The most successful radio programs jumped to the more lucrative medium of television, leaving radio with the least visual programming—music. People who have grown up with all-music radio are unaware that the past of radio includes a far greater diversity of programs. That about 90 percent of radio stations today do little more than play records for the bulk of their programming content is itself an example of pseudo-choice.

Early Top 40 formats embraced all types of popular music, including show tunes and country and western. The format at some stations became Top 60 with repetition of a "limited playlist" of the forty or sixty "top" songs. Today Top 40 exists in name only. Playlists of popular music stations are limited to twenty or even fifteen songs per week.

WLS is currently Chicago's most successful popular music station. The weekly rotation of songs totals only fifteen tunes. The top songs are selected by tabulating requests and surveying record stores in a five-state area. Only the taste of the majority is honored. The number one and number two songs of the week are played at one-hour intervals. Numbers three and four on the list are played every ninety minutes. The other eleven songs are played an average of one and a half times per DJ stint but have no preset order. The playing of the top four is carefully controlled by a digital clock that reminds the DJ every fifteen minutes that it is time for one of the big four.

Other AM radio formats are also tightly restricted, even though they play more than a dozen songs per week. Many "Beautiful Music" stations have prerecorded tapes shipped in from a central programming headquarters so that local outlets are little more than a tape recorder hooked to a transmitter.

Listeners have greater choice on the FM band today than on AM. FM now accounts for 36.4 percent of all radio listening in the top ten American cities according to a recent industry survey. In 1970, the figure was only 19 percent. During the prime-time seven to midnight hours, 50 percent of all radios are tuned to FM stations in many large cities. Some of the FM boom is a reaction to the obvious lack of choice offered by AM. The crossover is similar to that which occurred in the early 1960s when the major record companies severely restricted their offerings and almost missed the surge to rock music.

FM is currently a mecca of variety in large cities, an oasis where pseudo-choice appears but remains a distinct minority. However, the natural tendency of any medium that becomes big business is toward the offering of pseudo-choice. Time will tell if FM will succumb or remain a local outlet for audio creativity.

Radio, music, television and film are industries that deal in myth and yet are controlled by large corporations. Entertainment often consists in choosing the offerings of Gulf & Western or Warner Communications or Columbia. Entertainment becomes something provided by a corporation rather than something we invent to renew ourselves. Our myths cease to be vehicles for wisdom and truth and become instead a convenient way to increase corporate dividends and engineer pseudo-choices.

Chapter 8
Sport and the Virtue of Play

The worlds of play and sport take us into a realm of pseudo-choice different from the worlds of television, advertising, food and other aspects of everyday life we have already explored. In our introduction we described (but did not define) pseudo-choice as a decision made without an awareness of hidden forces at work shaping that selection. Our examination of pseudo-choice so far has dealt primarily with the engineers of decision who intentionally seek to influence our judgment to eat certain kinds of food, spend time in front of the TV tube, adopt the auto as an extension of ourselves or stay a few more minutes in the shopping center or grocery store.

The hidden factors in the world of sport and play are not obscured by clever engineers of deception; they are hidden because we have neglected the deeper meaning of sport and play. What is hidden in sports is the fact that spectators or players of the game are not merely killing time or exercising—they are participating in a newly created world.

A plot device often used in science fiction is the existence of a world parallel to earth. The device usually provides an earthman with a secret place or machine that enables him to transfer into the parallel world. One reason the device is used in the world of sci-fi is that it is plausible in Einsteinian space. Another reason is that the parallel world allows readers to fulfill in fantasy their natural desire to be able to switch worlds, and therefore identities, with the ease of a change in clothing. The other world is invariably one bearing striking similarities to earth, but possessing a few mind-bending differences. The interworld traveler returns to earth having learned a profound lesson about human existence—the parallel world thereby serves as a global experiment in human survival. When the traveler returns, he likely finds that his long sojourn (it could be for a generation or more) in the other world marked the passage of only a few minutes, or of no earth time at all.

If we translate this plot device to the sphere of human existence, we find that such universe swapping is more than sci-fi fantasy. The new world is not a globe spinning in some long-forgotten region of the galaxy; it is an experimental world where myth and magic thrive. It is the world of play and sport, and its existence is not confined to the clever use of metaphors; it is real.

A sporting event is one in which a crowd gathers to watch a select group of people step into the magic space defined by white stripes or black lines. In this world the ordinary universe dissolves and is replaced by the new world with its own time system, boundaries, rules, police, taboos, sacred areas, traditions, costumes, manners, gods, heroes and definitions of the ideal being.

The space (playing field, court, ring, etc.) in which sport takes place is a magical space similar in function to the primitive concept of sacred space. To ancient people not all space was equal; some was very special in that it allowed contact with the gods. These sacred areas, whether caves, mountains, temples or altars, were places where certain privileged beings could contact the gods. These places provided entrance to a different level of existence, a parallel world of sorts. Like both sacred space and sci-fi's "doorway-to-a-neighboring-universe," a playing field is carefully marked to represent entry to a different level of being. Those who step within its boundaries agree to accept the rules and laws of the game world.

Within the playing area normal time is suspended and a special time system and clock are used to mark progress. In many game worlds the time system is one that can be stopped when play ceases, unlike the unrelenting time outside the boundaries. Twenty minutes of time on a basketball court or football field can take an hour or more of earth time. Players lose track of real time while involved in the game world and often report having no idea if the game required thirty or sixty minutes to play.

Time in sports is again more like that experienced by primitive man—cyclical. Our New Year's celebration is a pale reflection of the ancient belief that history literally repeats itself. But that reflection is much clearer in sport where a gunshot, bell, buzzer or cry of an umpire marks the birth of the cosmos as well as its official demise. The sport world dies and is resurrected with each game and with each new season.

Inside the play world order reigns supreme even though chaos might rule outside. Players from the imperfect world enter the play territory and agree to follow strict and often arbitrary rules so that the world may function smoothly. Referees, umpires and judges are the supreme law and tribunal from where there is no higher judgment. In the sport world, rules are clear and well defined, unlike the laws of the ordinary world. A ball or strike in baseball is defined by the boundaries of the player's anatomy and home plate, but it is determined by the fiat of the umpire whose call may or may not correspond to the realities of physical space. Reality is determined by the police (umpires, referees, judges), and the players accept this imperfection in the name of order. Real-world technology could supply machines that call balls or strikes or determine field goals or extra points with unerring sonar accuracy—but the sport world prefers to allow a mere mortal to control the law. These game police are unarmed men who often must rule those nearly twice their size. The game police hold the ultimate weapon; they can ban players from the universe—for a time. There is a rule book for every sport such as does not exist for the real world.

This parallel universe of play has no professional rule breakers. There is crime but no hardened criminals. A constant rule breaker is a spoil sport. A basketball player who refuses to dribble or a baseball player who runs from first to third via the pitcher's mound cannot survive his criminal ways. Crimes are detected, tried and judged on the spot and punishment is swift and nearly always befits the crime.

The play world has differences in styles but no radicals. The revolutionary athlete might question the basic assumptions of the society outside the playing field, but once he steps across the boundary into the play world he does not theorize if, for example, placing a ball through a hoop is a valid basis for basketball—he accepts these givens without question.

Within the physical space of the playing field or court there are areas, as in the world outside, that are sacred or taboo. A player in basketball may not stay more than three seconds in the foul zone without penalty; only one individual has the privilege of touching the soccer ball in the box by the goal. The golf green is governed by different rules than the fairway and both differ from the rough or hazards. Nonplayers are forbidden access to the playground, and to play the game one should wear the proper costume.

The costumes are not needed to make the world of sport function, but like the related worlds of the stage and screen, they add to the specialness of the separate world to aid the spectators (and players) in the suspension of disbelief. The athlete's uniform, the priestly vestments, the soldier's uniform, the actor's makeup, the warrior's face paint all serve the same purpose: they symbolize and make more real the entrance into a different world.

The world of play is not one of make-believe—it is as real as any other world. The fact that it can be created by whim and ended by a buzzer does not mean it is unreal. All the emotions of the outside world can be found in the world of play, but more intense and more frequent; there are success and failure even unto death. Johan Huizinga, in his classic study of play, *Homo Ludens*, demonstrates that civilization (another name for that "real" world) springs from play. He says, "The spirit of playful competition is, as a social impulse, older than culture itself and pervades all life like a veritable ferment. Ritual grew up in sacred play; poetry was born in play; music and dancing were pure play. . . . The rules of warfare, the conventions of noble living were built up on play-patterns. Even our legal system functions much as a contest between opposing teams."

Huizinga defines play as ". . . a free activity standing quite consciously outside ordinary life as being not serious, but at the same time absorbing the player intensely and utterly." This idea of play admits the possibility that religious ritual is a kind of play as is art. Play is not a frivolous means of escape; it is rather an opportunity for a person to be fully human. It is this opportunity for full humanity that is most often hidden from view, making the play decision at least partially a pseudo-choice.

The decision to enter the sportsworld is a pseudo-choice to the extent that the player is unable or unwilling to leave one universe and enter another. The word "sport" is a shortened form of "disport," a Latin-rooted word meaning "to carry away." The person unable to become "carried away" to this parallel universe defined by special rules, time and boundaries is not engaging in sport. The universe of sport is not entered when the joyful spirit of play is replaced by sport as big business, sport as a way to avoid an early heart attack or to stay slim or sport as a chance to buy the flashiest equipment, wear the proper clothes and gain entry to a desirable status elite. To the extent that such considerations motivate the "player," he or she is more an intruder than a participant in the parallel universe. The only baggage needed to enter sportsworld is the spirit of play.

The spirit of play was a much more important and integral part of primitive man than it is today. Today we have fragmented play from the rest of life instead of allowing the spirit of play to infuse all of life. The current American attitude toward work and play is ambiguous to the point of schizophrenia. As a nation, we feel somewhat guilty about devoting a large amount of time to play, yet we pay play-experts in sports and entertainment the highest salaries. We speak of the right to work and its inherent dignity and consider "playing around" a waste of valuable time suitable only for children who are not ready to make more valuable contributions.

While burning vigil lights at the shrine of "noble work," our worship is distracted by dreams of a land with no labor where we would be free to play. Work is most often thought of as that which we do almost grudgingly; if we enjoy an activity and engage in it for its own sake, such is not work. Work is both valued and dreaded; play is both sought and looked upon as valuable only to enable a person to work more effectively.

Play was once accepted as the ideal state of living; work was viewed as a necessary evil. Today, we have almost completely reversed this view. Play is tolerated especially for those not capable of working; but to be "playing around" is to be wasting time which is as valuable as money. Time is to be "spent" in transforming the earth through work, which is, after all, humanity's mission on this planet.

One of the causes of such a confused outlook is an idea rather recently arrived on the time line of world history: that work is intrinsically valuable. Americans certainly do believe in the value of work as an end in itself. Calvin Coolidge might be most remembered in regard to work for his immortal comment that "When more and more people are thrown out of work, unemployment results," but he did sum up the ideals of a nation when he stated that "Work is not a curse, it is the prerogative of intelligence, the only means to manhood, and the measures of civilization. Savages do not work."

This exaltation of the concept of work is relatively new in human history. The Biblical view of work that has most penetrated our national consciousness is that not of a "right" to be demanded, but rather of a punishment to be accepted in the face of Adam and Eve's original failing. Most Paradises, Golden Ages and Heavens of the past are places of no work at all—they are magnificent playgrounds. If one goes back far enough, history shows that for ancient man the concept of work didn't even exist. Many primitive societies have no words in their vocabulary to distinguish between work and play. Such primitive people have not fragmented their lives into compartments of play activities and work activities. They live in depth, neither working nor playing—they simply live.

For more recent historical man, work is at best a necessary evil. Hesiod in *Works and Days* finds work a curse; Socrates in *Xenophon* views work as merely an expedient. Aristotle saw the greatest value of work in its capacity to provide the leisuretime which is the true base of civilization.

It would seem that the concept of work as good for the soul first came through the Benedictine monks who believed that "idleness is the enemy of the soul" and that manual labor is beneficial for the monks. The spiritual discipline of work spread until the whole world became a monastery and every man a monk. Even today we speak of the trade manual of a profession as its "bible" and speak of working at a job "religiously." Work today remains as a quasi-religious value. To shirk work is to avoid religious duty, to be without a job is to be excommunicated from society as a social misfit, to have "nothing to do" is to feel pangs of guilt.

Even our sense of identity is partly determined by the work we do. When asked, "Who are you?" a person (especially in our culture, a man) normally thinks first of his name and secondly of his job. We say, "He *is* a bricklayer, he *is* a secretary, she *is* an accountant." In other words, in many ways a person is what he or she does. Self-identity is achieved through work. So, for a man to be unemployed is to be lacking an integral part of his own identity. It is not enough for wholeness to be a man; one must, in our society, be a workingman.

There is no danger in bestowing upon work a profound dignity; the problem arises when such exaltation is given to an incomplete concept of work. An examination of the activities that most people feel belong to the sphere of work shows that work is thought of as activity that does not require the involvement of the entire person.

A strenuous game of baseball or touch football is only play because the entire person is involved in the activity. A much less strenuous activity, such as stocking grocery shelves or piecework on an assembly line, is thought of solely as work because it involves only a part of a person. Work is thought of as an activity in which a person is fragmented rather than unified through the use of all faculties.

This fragmenting of the person and using only part at a time makes for boredom and dissatisfaction, for humans are not created to be used as a machine, one part at a time. In a machine, unused parts last longer and add life. In a person, unused faculties, mind or body, result in atrophy and turn the individual more into a machine than a human person.

The distinction between work and play for a person totally involved in action becomes meaningless. Such a person feels no guilt about what others call play, is not bored and does not dread "going to work," feels no constant need to get away from work and is usually both happy and productive. Many business executives amaze people by their capacity for work even when they reach the stage of financial independence and no longer need to work for a living. These are people who find their "work" completely involving and who, when asked, might claim that they really don't divide their lives into work and play categories. They do not view their activity as work any more than does a game player who really enjoys the game he or she is playing. The workaholic sins not by dedication to work but obsession and complete self-identification with only one facet of existence.

Those who demand the right to work really want the right to income. Perhaps it would be more beneficial to demand the right to play. For the greatest danger in our concept of work is not that we value it too highly but rather that it neglects, even demeans, the profound value of play. For it is in play that a person is totally involved, it is in play that a person is most human. The freedom and involvement of the player have contributed much to society. Many great inventions were the result of playing with ideas; the word "play" is used in love and sex to express well the involvement of two people with each other; the person at play loses track of time and the player in a game lives in depth in the world of the game.

Social historian Eric Hoffer points out that almost every utilitarian device had its beginning in a nonutilitarian pursuit or pastime. The puppy dog was the first domesticated animal not because it was the most useful, but because it was most playful. He points out that it is plausible that planting and irrigating, the invention of the wheel, sailing, brickmaking, etc. were invented in the course of play. The Aztecs did not have the wheel, but their toy animals had rollers for feet. Hoffer observes that ornaments preceded clothing and that the bow was a musical instrument before it became a weapon.

Play can accurately be described as humanity's most useful occupation. In *The Ordeal of Change* Hoffer points out that ". . . it is imperative to keep in mind that man painted, engraved, carved and modeled long before he made a pot, wove cloth, worked metals or domesticated an animal." The artist and the player came before the utilitarian and the worker.

Today, adults and play simply don't go together. To accuse an individual of merely playing at his job is grounds for dismissal. A student who plays is one who shirks responsibility for the work of learning. A wife never tells her husband what she might command her children to do: "Go out and play." Children have playrooms, adults have workshops—yet the activity engaged in in both is sometimes distinguishable only by the quality of the finished product.

Many adults feel guilty about playing for long periods of time. They become restless and desire to "get back to work" while complaining of "nothing to do." The standard view is that play has the task of enabling us to recover from the adverse effects of work and to prepare to work better after vacationing in America's playgrounds.

Play is first of all a free activity. Play and force simply do not go together. Play is never imposed by duty, it is done during leisure, at a "free" time. It is this freedom that removes from the player inhibitions to creativity. Toying with an idea in a playful manner is often more effective than "working" at a problem. A society that stresses work above play risks stifling the freedom necessary for creativity.

In play, freedom and creativity merge to produce art. The art of drama is expressed in a *play* performed by *players*, music is *played* on some instrument, philosophy is the art of *playing* with ideas and poetry is *playing* with words. A person who is unable to play, to enter the sport/play universe on its own terms can experience only a very limited degree of freedom.

To watch a person at play is to see into the soul; you are how you play. To watch a person cope with the problems of tennis, golf, volleyball or any one of dozens of other sports is to watch a person reveal his or her deepest values and philosophy of living. And to observe a nation at play is to learn about its sociology and self-concept.

Sport and games are expressive of the players and the society in which they thrive. They serve as a mass medium which both projects and reflects values. Chess is as perfect a mirror of medieval life idealized as Monopoly is of the capitalist society, and Scrabble and crossword puzzles of a literate society.

This aspect of sport as a separate universe helps explain why taboo-breaking books such as *Ball Four*, *Out of Their League* or *The Jocks* were greeted with shock and derision. These books said that sports figures really aren't gods at all. They are ordinary human beings with failings like the rest of us. Such a message might be true, but it shatters the separate world that spectators and fans need and want. So sportswriters know that the truth is not what is demanded; what is appreciated is writing that strengthens the myth. Fans want the Four Horsemen of the Apocalypse to populate the backfield and Bionic Ballet to fill the basketball court. Ordinary mortals are permitted only as a necessary evil.

Sport is a ritual, an acting out of a myth or series of myths. A sport that can be considered a national pastime can be expected to reflect national values and wishes. Sports that capture the national fancy are ritualistic enactments of the American Dream. Baseball is still called our national pastime but is rapidly being replaced by American football. That football should become our "national pastime" is understandable to those who can see sports as reflections of national character.

American football is passionately concerned with the gain and loss of land, of territory. The football field is measured and marked with all the care of a surveyor and the ball's progress noted to the nearest inch. Football is a precise game and its players are often trained like a military unit on a mission to gain territory for the mother country. The players are the popular heroes but the coaches and owners run the game, using the players to carry out their plans—there is comparatively little room for individual initiative. A score comes as the result of a strategic series of well-executed manuevers and is bought on the installment plan, yard by yard.

The regulation and almost military precision of American football is a reflection of national psychology. Even the words we use to describe the game include throwing the bomb, marching downfield, game plan (which has become nearly a national phrase for any field, from selling toothpaste to covering up political scandals), guards, executions, blitz, zone, platoon, squad, drills, attack, drives, marching bands for entertainment, stars on helmets, lines that can be blasted through and even war paint. Much of the verbal similarity comes from the fact that war was originally the ultimate game played within the confines of certain rules agreed upon by both "teams."

Football, more than any other sport, is a game for spectators to watch superhuman, mythical heroes. Football is a sport that more people watch than play. The game requires too many people, too much space and is simply too dangerous for the weekend athlete. The size and speed of professional players and their uniforms make them into heroic figures capable of feats that invite admiration but not imitation. The football spectator is in awe of the armored monsters. The viewer of a golf match or even baseball or tennis dreams of going out the next day and doing likewise, but football is played only by the gods who can run the 100 yard dash in ten seconds, stand six feet three and weigh 260 pounds.

The demise of baseball as our national pastime reflects a change in national character. The change does not mean the disappearance of baseball, merely its relocation to a position as just another game rather than *the* game. Professor John Finlay of the University of Manitoba, writing in *Queen's Quarterly*, compares baseball to an acting out of the robber baron stage of capitalism, whereas football more clearly reflects a more mature capitalism into which we are now moving. Hence, the rise in popularity of football and apparent decline in baseball. He notes that Japan, still in the early stages of capitalism, has taken avidly to baseball but not to football. It is not a question of Japanese physique serving as a determinant since rugby has a large Asian following. He predicts that when their capitalism moves into a higher stage, the Japanese will move on to football as have Americans.

Baseball is a game of a quieter age when less action was needed to hold interest, when going to the park was enjoyable (baseball is still played in ball parks while football is played in stadiums), when aggression was subservient to finesse. Baseball players did not need exposure as college players to succeed as football players do; they play a relatively calm game almost daily instead of a bruising gladiatorial contest weekly. Baseball has room for unique and colorful characters, while football stresses the more anonymous but effective team member. Baseball is a game in which any team can win at any given contest and there are no favorites; only football has real "upsets." Football's careful concern with time adds a tension to the game that is lacking in the more leisurely world of baseball.

Football has replaced baseball as the favorite American spectator sport largely because of television. A comparison between a telecast of a football game on one channel and a baseball game on another would reveal baseball as a game with people standing around seemingly with little to do but watch two men play catch. Football would appear as twenty-two men engaged in almost constant, frenzied action. To watch baseball requires identification with the home team; to watch football requires only a need for action or a week of few thrills and the need for a touch of vicarious excitement.

Baseball is a pastoral game, timeless and highly ritualized; its appeal is to nostalgia and so might enjoy periods of revitalization in comparison to football. But for now, the myth of football suits the nation better.

According to a 1974 Harris survey, baseball has already been statistically dethroned. In a sports survey a cross section of nearly fourteen hundred fans was asked, "Which of these sports do you follow?"

	1974 %	1973 %	1972 %	1971 %
Football	63	65	67	60
Baseball	58	62	60	57
Basketball	44	46	42	46
Tennis	26	17	16	11
Auto racing	24	26	23	22
Golf	24	28	20	23
Bowling	23	28	27	27
Horse racing	20	18	18	17
Boxing	19	29	22	31
Track & field	19	21	23	18
Hockey	16	22	22	17

The decision to play or "follow" a certain sport is also the decision to live a certain myth. The team violence of football, the craftiness of basketball, the mechanistic precision of bowling, the auto racer's devotion to machinery are all subworlds within the universe of sport.

Golf, for example, is a unique subworld, one of the few left as a sport (unlike hunting which does not involve scoring or teams) in which the game is played between man and nature. The winner of a match is one who has beaten the opponent, but the game itself is a person versus the environment. To understand the appeal of golf it is again necessary to consider the game as a ritual reenactment of an appealing myth.

Golf, perhaps more than any other sport, has to be played to be appreciated. Millions who never played football can enjoy the game on TV, but only a dedicated participant can sit through two hours of televised golf. Golf is growing in participation but still has the stigma of an upper-class game. Eighty percent of the nation's golfers must play on 20 percent of the nation's courses that are open to the public. The ratio of public to private facilities hurts public participation in the game but mirrors the inequities of society and provides a convenient status symbol for those who can afford club membership. Its TV audience is not the largest of any sport but it is the most well heeled.

Golf is a reenactment of the pioneer spirit. It is man versus a hostile environment in search of an oasis. The goal is a series of lush "greens," each protected by natural hazards such as water, sand and unmanageably long grass. The hazards are no threat to physical life but they are to the achievement of success. Golf is a journey game with a constantly changing field. Golfers start the eighteen-hole journey, can rest at a halfway point and then resume until they return to near the point of origination.

The winner of the match is one who has fallen victim to the fewest hazards and overcome the terrain. Many golf courses have Indian names as if to remind the golfer of the frontier ethos. A local course called Indian Lakes invites golfers to use either one of two courses—the Iroquois trail or the Sioux trail.

Golf, like baseball, is a pastoral sport—with a high degree of tensions and drama but relatively little action. It is a game in which players are constantly in awe of the magic flight of the golf ball. To hit any kind of ball 100 or 200 or more yards with accuracy or to hit a small target from 150 yards is an amazing feat to be appreciated only by those who have at least tried the game. Golf is very likely the most difficult game to master, yet one in which the average player occasionally hits a shot as good as the best of any professional. It is this dream of magic results that keeps the golfer on course.

To look amid the myths of each sport for one that best suits our national character is to search in vain. Perhaps it is best to say that the sport that is most played is our national myth, or that which is most watched and enjoyed. Football is most watched but seldom played. But there is an activity that characterizes our nation in sport and that is "spectating." Certainly we are, more than any nation in history, a nation of spectators.

One need not be an athlete to participate in the myth of the sport. All that is needed is a local team or a handy television set. Television enables spectators to share vicariously in the drama enacted in the mythical world of the playing field. Each year the three networks (this does not count local sports programs) will beam one thousand hours of sports coverage to receptive audiences. Aside from a few blockbuster movies, sports programs are the most watched of any television offerings. A Super Bowl game reaches about half the households in the nation—that is seventy million people, more than belong to any one religion or more than vote for a President.

These seventy million are, to borrow a phrase from sports journalist William Johnson, superspectators snared by the electric lilliputians who move on the glass tube. These eighteen-inch quarterbacks and foot-high tennis stars shape the nation's choices in sport. What is televised is what people play; the variety of the sportsworld is described in *TV Guide* listings for the weekends and Monday night.

Televised sports help shape the offerings of school athletic departments. Schools devote an overwhelming amount of time, energy and money to sports that few students will play past the age of thirty, or even twenty. In spite of lip service paid in written philosophies about educating the whole person and preparing the student for the adult world, school sports mirror the business world. Whichever professional sport has captured the nation's fancy is the one that captures the school's energies—football and basketball are currently the top two. A handful of the best students compete while the majority of the students either avoid sports completely or participate as spectators.

Schools have not yet offered courses in remedial sports. They work on the assumption that some students simply are not "athletic" enough or well-coordinated enough to enjoy sports. There is little attempt made to teach coordination or physical skills. Those with ability enjoy the "physical education" class, those without are humiliated and learn to stay in the stands. Winning and work have replaced play and fun. Schools offer students a pseudo-choice: either utter devotion to winning or benign neglect leading to an adult unable to enjoy trips into the world of sport except as a spectator.

The hidden message of the athletic department in schools is that sports are for the best players while others should become spectators. And students learn this lesson well.

Spectating is not inherently evil or dehumanizing; rather it is a somewhat instinctive human activity. The words passive and spectator are often strung together by critics. Strange how opera lovers and museum strollers are never criticized for "passive spectating." But when it becomes an obsession, a substitute for participation, then it is at least a symptom if not a cause for a failure to realize one's human potential. New York Knickerbockers forward Bill Bradley explained the feeling of being used by spectators: "Thousands of people who don't know me use my participation on a Sunday afternoon as an excuse for non-action, as a fix to help them escape their everyday problems and our society's problems. The toll of providing that experience is beginning to register on me."

But the toll of being a full-time spectator can also be trying. In 1973 a Colorado man shot himself in the head after watching the Denver Broncos fumble a half-dozen times in a single game. His suicide note explained, "I have been a Broncos' fan since the Broncos were first organized and I can't stand their fumbling any more." That he should attack himself and not the fumbling football players indicates that he viewed himself as a participant in the games.

Spectators do not "watch" games, not the true fan (a word that comes from fanatic but tempts one to consider "fantasy" as a root); he or she participates. The idea of a home team goes back to the Greek city-states but has survived even in our mobile society. The fact that the twentieth-century home team is little more than a group of hired mercenaries (even in college) matters little—the illusion works. Media control of sport threatens the specter of a football game in which the stands are emptied by no-shows and the game is played like a drama on a movie set or a rehearsal in an empty auditorium. But the TV cameras beam the game to millions at home who root for their own version of the good guys to win.

There is beauty in watching sport; there is also education. Many minor sports have audiences composed primarily of those who participate in the sport and have come to watch the experts play in the hopes of both admiring but also learning. One suspects golf and tennis crowds are also players of those sports. But the beauty and the education are not enough. Dance is a beautiful series of movements (bearing some relation to sports like basketball and football), but it arouses less enthusiasm in the nation than all but a few sports. It is necessary in sport, as in drama and film, that the spectators identify with the action and thus experience vicarious emotions.

Thus, the best players become as gods, mythical heroes whose exploits we share and about whom we eagerly read every detail of his or her personal life. Half the men who read the morning paper look first and only to the sports section. They do not want news, they want their heroes to be praised, they want their beliefs strengthened. There is invincibility, poor people can become rich, there are giants in the world and beasts disguised as humans. David can sometimes beat Goliath, Zeus still hurls no-hitters and Mercury can gain a thousand yards at the Sunday worship gathering.

The players are abstractions of speed, strength, power or grace under pressure. They are the qualities we once had when young or the qualities we never had but like a child who wants someday to become a ballplayer we dream about having. We are Clark Kent but our heroes are supermen.

The athlete as a demigod was not created by the mass media although they encourage it partly because it is "what the people want" and partly because it is exploitable. The athlete is a god because sport is myth in action and the spectator is a vicarious participant. We have already seen how the advertisers exploit sport as myth to further the engineering of pseudo-choices in the marketplace. Perhaps the increase in spectator sport is part of the reason for a recent increase in sport participation. Watching others play makes us also want to enter the universe.

There is a wave of participation as a life-style that has swept the nation. Worshipers demand to take part in church services instead of assuming the roles of silent spectators, students want a share in running the school, businesses allow greater employee participation in corporate planning, even sports spectators are more likely to streak across the field or throw an egg or a snowball. An A. C. Nielsen survey reveals that 62 percent of households have at least one member who swims, 47 percent include a person who fishes, 21 percent, a boater, 46 percent, a cyclist, about a third include someone who bowls or plays pool and nearly one in five includes a person who plays tennis or golf. People are not content to sit and watch the pros on television.

Competition is an integral part of sportsworld, yet it is a value under question by a new generation of players. To compete is sometimes seen as to enjoy the misfortune of others and to mirror the dog-eat-dog philosophy of the business world. Why not play games that teach cooperation instead of competition? these new thinkers ask. Since games both teach and reflect social values, could not new games based on competition teach a more humane way of living? Must all sports teach that success is "beating" some other person or group? Isn't the military and the drive to be "number one" in the world connected to this obsession with winning and competing?

Yet even the most gentle and nonviolent of persons enjoy competition. There seems to be something almost instinctive about competing and there is hardly a culture in the world that does not have some form of ritualized competition.

Perhaps the problem can never be solved by eliminating the urge to compete. Stewart Brand, who gained fame by producing the *Whole Earth Catalog*, organized a new games tournament partly because of frustration with Vietnam. "I felt that American combat was being pushed as far away as the planet would allow, becoming abstract and remote, and it suggested to me that there was something wrong with our conflict forms here." So the combative instinct needs more outlets for the increasing desire to participate. Perhaps the puzzling degeneration of the behavior of fans at gatherings from rock concerts to baseball games has something to do with a lack of participatory outlets. We need to contact and confront our own competitive urges rather than deny them either by an exclusive emphasis on games of cooperation or by allowing professionals to perform our sports. Sport and sex have much in common, but we have yet to allow professionals to satisfy our need for sex. Sex has yet to become a spectator sport to the exclusion of participation.

Yet we have emphasized the results of the contest rather than its execution, the winning over the playing. Ballet and basketball are similar in many ways but no one would consider keeping score in ballet or playing basketball without a scoring system. There is so much concentration on the final score that sometimes the beauty of sport is lost. The sports page more closely resembles the stock market listing than a compendium of descriptions of beautiful human activity.

What sport needs, in order to ensure that its players can fully choose its separate universe, is an increase in the available outlets for the average person and a greater realization of the value of playing the game for its own sake. Sport needs emphasis on the spirit of play, but not an elimination of competition.

The athlete who measures performance in percentages, won/lost records, statistics and scores chances a loss of sport as a magical, humanizing experience. Only recently are players, professional and amateur alike, rediscovering that winning isn't everything. To the extent that extrinsic rewards, such as money and statistical excellence, become the goals and standards of a sport, the intrinsic joy of the game is diminished. The pseudo-choice of sport without play leaves a gap, an absence of the deeper joy of the game.

It is fitting to conclude this book with a chapter on sport and the virtue of play. Having spent so much of our time in the world of the marketplace and in coping with daily necessities, it is useful to remember that there are deeper needs that pseudo-choices leave untouched. Life itself, as Plato reminded us, must be lived as play.

Index